Business Law

21st
CENTURY
BUSINESS

SECOND EDITION

John E. Adamson

• Jurisdiction is the ability to call shots - courts have the power to hear and decide cases
  - Original jurisdiction - first to hear case
  ← Appellate jurisdiction - reviews transcripts (verbatem record)

GUROBLZHFGYVIR

SOUTH-WESTERN
CENGAGE Learning™

Australia • Brazil • Japan • Korea • Mexico • Singapore • Spain • United Kingdom • United States

SOUTH-WESTERN
CENGAGE Learning™

21st Century Business
Business Law, 2nd Edition
John E. Adamson

Editorial Director: Jack W. Calhoun

Vice President/Editor-in-Chief: Karen Schmohe

Executive Editor: Eve Lewis

Senior Developmental Editor: Penny Shank

Editorial Assistant: Anne Kelly

Marketing Manager: Diane Morgan

Technology Project Manager: Lysa Kosins

Content Project Management: Pre-Press PMG

Senior Manufacturing Buyer: Kevin Kluck

Production Service: Pre-Press PMG

Senior Art Director: Tippy McIntosh

Internal Design: Pre-Press PMG

Cover Designer: Lou Ann Thesing

Cover Image: Getty Images, iStock

Permission Acquisitions Manager/Text:
 Mardell Glinkski-Schultz

Permission Acquisitions Manager/Photo:
 Deanna Ettinger

For product information and technology assistance, contact us at
Cengage Learning Customer & Sales Support, 1-800-354-9706

For permission to use material from this text or product,
submit all requests online at **www.cengage.com/permissions**
Further permissions questions can be emailed to
permissionrequest@cengage.com

Exam*View*® is a registered trademark of eInstruction Corp. Windows is a registered trademark of the Microsoft Corporation used herein under license. Macintosh and Power Macintosh are registered trademarks of Apple Computer, Inc. used herein under license.

© 2008 Cengage Learning. All Rights Reserved.

Library of Congress Control Number: 2009943304

Student Edition ISBN 13: 978-0-538-74061-6

Student Edition ISBN 10: 0-538-74061-2

South-Western Cengage Learning
5191 Natorp Boulevard
Mason, OH 45040
USA

Cengage Learning products are represented in Canada by Nelson Education, Ltd.

For your course and learning solutions, visit **school.cengage.com**

Printed in the United States of America
2 3 4 5 16 15 14 13

The *21st Century Business Series* is an innovative instructional program providing instructors with the greatest flexibility to deliver business content using a modular format. Instructors can create their own business courses by combining several **Learner Guides** in the *Series* to form one-semester or two-semester courses. The individual **Learner Guides** can also be used as enhancements to more traditional business courses or to tailor new courses to meet emerging needs.

The design and content of each **Learner Guide** in the *21st Century Business Series* is engaging yet easy for students to use. The content focuses on providing opportunities for applying 21st Century business skills while enabling innovative learning methods that integrate the use of supportive technology and creative problem-solving approaches in today's business world.

The *Business Law* **Learner Guide** covers today's most relevant business topics, including disposition of property after death or divorce. Short case studies followed by critical thinking questions are included in each chapter allowing students to demonstrate their grasp on each chapter's topic.

ORGANIZED FOR SUCCESS

Each chapter opens with a **Project** that incorporates information from each lesson within the chapter. These **Projects** pull all of the information from the chapter together so students get a hands-on experience applying what they learned, making for a great group activity.

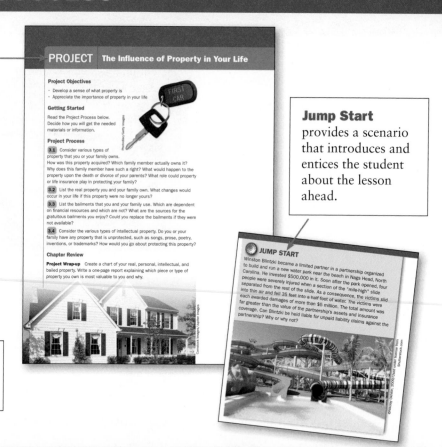

Net Bookmark gives chapter-related activities for students to complete using information found on the Internet.

Jump Start provides a scenario that introduces and entices the student about the lesson ahead.

REAL-WORLD FOCUS

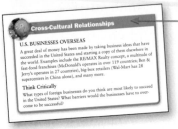

Cross-Cultural Relationships highlights the importance of understanding and respecting everyone's point of view and thinking about the perspectives of others.

Tech Literacy highlights how evolving technology plays a huge role in how business is conducted.

In each chapter, you will find a **Use Your Judgment** feature followed by **Think Critically**. These features give students an example and questions that apply to the material within the chapter and allow students to either answer the questions on their own or participate in a group discussion.

Teamwork provides an activity that requires the students to work together as a team.

HANDS-ON LEARNING

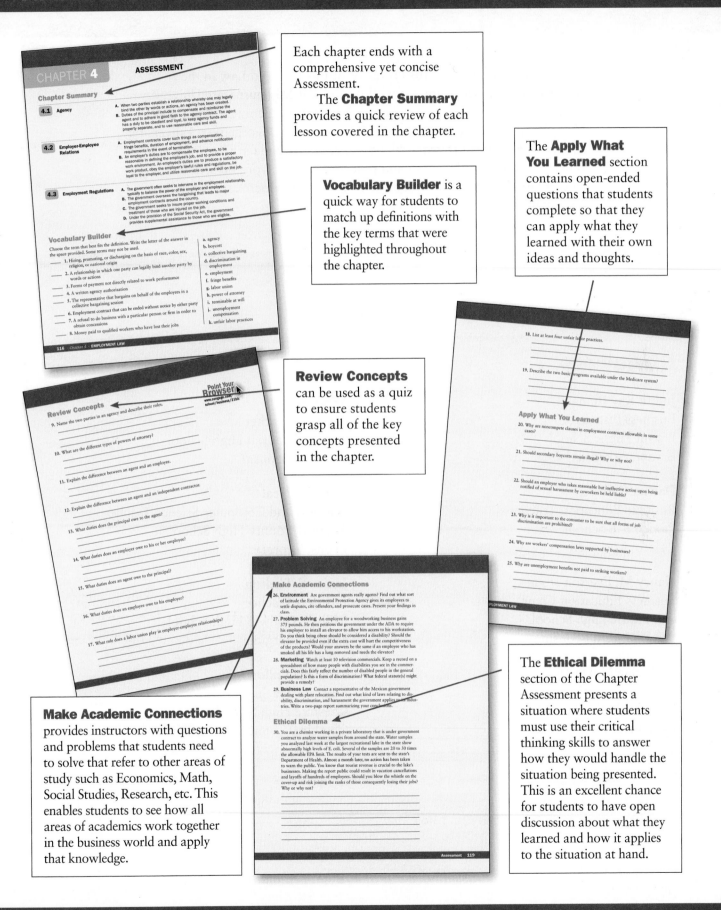

Each chapter ends with a comprehensive yet concise Assessment.

The **Chapter Summary** provides a quick review of each lesson covered in the chapter.

Vocabulary Builder is a quick way for students to match up definitions with the key terms that were highlighted throughout the chapter.

The **Apply What You Learned** section contains open-ended questions that students complete so that they can apply what they learned with their own ideas and thoughts.

Review Concepts can be used as a quiz to ensure students grasp all of the key concepts presented in the chapter.

Make Academic Connections provides instructors with questions and problems that students need to solve that refer to other areas of study such as Economics, Math, Social Studies, Research, etc. This enables students to see how all areas of academics work together in the business world and apply that knowledge.

The **Ethical Dilemma** section of the Chapter Assessment presents a situation where students must use their critical thinking skills to answer how they would handle the situation being presented. This is an excellent chance for students to have open discussion about what they learned and how it applies to the situation at hand.

ABOUT THE AUTHOR

John E. Adamson is Emeritus Professor of Business and Law in the Department of Finance and General Business at Missouri State University. Adamson received a B.S. from the U.S. Military Academy at West Point, New York; an M.A. in International Relations from Georgetown University; and an M.B.A. and J.D. from the University of Virginia at Charlottesville. A decorated, disabled veteran and past four-term mayor and school board member of his hometown, Adamson is author of numerous business law texts, with a concentration on environmental law.

Reviewers

Judith Kay Binns
Business Instructor
Bryant Public Schools
Bryant, Arkansas

Dawna Carter
Business Education Teacher
Puxico R-8 School
Puxico, Missouri

Nancy M. Everson
Business Education Chair
Sun Prairie High School
Sun Prairie, Wisconsin

Catherine McDonald
Business Senior Teacher
Ridgefield High School
Ridgefield, Connecticut

Vicki Noss
Business Teacher
Beloit Memorial High School
Beloit, Wisconsin

Kathy O'Neal
Business and Computer Science Teacher
Toombs County High School
Lyons, Georgia

Janice B. Shelton
Business Teacher
Mills E. Godwin High School
Henrico, Virginia

Lynn M. Taillon
Business Teacher
Cheshire High School
Cheshire, Connecticut

CONTENTS

CHAPTER 1

Law and Justice

1.1 Law, Justice, and Ethics

1.2 Types of U.S. Law

1.3 Federal and State Legal Systems

Careers in Business Law

overnment & Public Administration

U.S. DEPARTMENT OF JUSTICE

Even during economic downturns, the federal government is one of the few sectors that continues to hire. New workers are always needed for the "mission critical" jobs of the various government departments and agencies. Many of these jobs require a working knowledge of the law.

Among the jobs in the Department of Justice is Paralegal Specialist. The U.S. Attorneys Office in the Department of Justice hires Paralegal Specialists to relieve attorneys of routine work assignments, such as drafting summons and proposing offers and settlements. Paralegal Specialists also assist attorneys in discovery procedures and investigations. They provide information concerning facts, issues, and case law.

To qualify for this position, candidates who already work for the government must have attained a certain job level. Those not employed by the government must have two full years of graduate-level education, such as masters or law degrees.

Think Critically

1. What job skills do you think are needed by Paralegal Specialists?
2. Does the Paralegal Specialist job interest you? Why or why not?

Project Objectives

- View the legal system at work
- Help distinguish among the various levels of the legal system
- Identify the laws involved in a specific case and their intended objectives

Comstock Images/Jupiter Images

Getting Started

Read the Project Process below. Make a list of any materials you will need.

- Go through the government section of your phone book and make a list of the various courts and governmental agencies in your area.
- Call them to find out if, when, and under what conditions their proceedings are open to the public. If the proceedings are open, make a list of upcoming cases and the issues to be determined in each.

Project Process

1.1 Attend at least an hour of a court trial or hearing in your area. Research the dispute and then discuss how each party involved might define "justice." Identify the ethical issues involved.

1.2 Research the history of the laws to be applied in the cases at hand. What is the source of each law? Note especially the intent behind the laws.

1.3 What is the overall jurisdiction of the court trying the case? Could the case have been brought before a different court or agency?

Chapter Review

Project Wrap-up   Evaluate the effectiveness of the legal system by answering the following questions about the case: Did the laws achieve their intended purpose? What were the expectations of each party to a case as to justice? Did the court and other parts of the legal system act properly?

Comstock Images/Jupiter Images

JUMP START

Ben and Bernice were driving to the local mall when a traffic officer stopped them. When Bernice asked what the offense was, the officer indicated that it was just a routine check. If the traffic officer stopped this driver because of his youthful appearance, has the officer acted lawfully? Would your answer change if the officer stated that the action was taken because drivers under age 25 account for 28 percent of fatal accidents but only comprise 13 percent of licensed drivers? Would you consider the officer's actions immoral? Why or why not?

Photodisc/Getty Images

Law and Justice

What is the law? *Black's Law Dictionary* uses more than a full page to define it. For your study of law in this course, it is best to use the basic definition: **Laws** are rules of conduct that a political authority will enforce.

Obviously, the law may take different forms depending on the situation in which it may be employed. You may meet it firsthand in the form of a highway patrol officer personalizing a ticket for you. As a businessperson, you may feel its watchful eye as it regulates your workplace and products and, inevitably, assesses taxes. The key point to realize is that proper laws and their evenhanded enforcement are essential to producing a stable environment within which business can succeed.

Business law refers to the specific group of laws that regulates the establishment, operation, and termination of commercial enterprises. Without a stable body of business laws, a businessperson would have to contend with many conflicting laws that would make profitable trade improbable, if not impossible. Nonetheless, a working knowledge of all aspects of the law, not just the specific area of business law, is required for your success.

The Growth of Law

In order to understand law and justice in society today, you must first know how the law developed. According to those who study the development of civilizations, most societies go through four stages when forming their legal systems.

Stage 1 In the first stage, injuries inflicted on one human being by another *Private acts of revenge* are assumed to be matters for personal revenge. Those who are wronged feel that an appropriate payback can be achieved only through directly punishing the wrongdoers. Gang-related shootings in our inner cities often are a result of this type of attitude. Such incidents usually disrupt the normal routine of the people and result in harm to innocent bystanders. The chaotic situation that results often leads to one individual seizing power and exerting a firm control to bring stability to the society.

Stage 2 This individual (called the *sovereign* or ruler) then brings about the second stage in the evolution of law. The sovereign does this by creating an alternative to personal revenge. This is typically in the form of a King's Court where parties can seek their revenge for wrongs done to them by appealing to the sovereign to punish the wrongdoer. The parties appear in the sovereign's court and accept awards of money or goods as a substitute for that revenge. *Civil law*

Stage 3 As the demands to appear in the sovereign's court grow, the sovereign typically responds by forming a system of courts to provide greater access for all. In this stage, elders or priests empowered by the sovereign sit in the sovereign's place to decide cases. The sovereign's subjects can go to the *Criminal law* courts to be heard when they are injured by another in some way. Eventually, the sovereign makes private acts of revenge illegal. This forces wronged parties to seek satisfaction in the sovereign's courts for the harms done to them.

Stage 4 Finally, the sovereign uses the law to prevent the wrongs from arising in the first place. These wrongs, from theft to assault to murder, are made crimes and become punishable by the sovereign through the court system. This is the fourth, and typically last, stage in the evolution of law. *— creation of punishable crimes*

What role does the court system play in obtaining justice?

Comstock Images/Jupiter Images

Justice

Justice is considered to be what is right, fair, or appropriate, based on one person's perspective, in response to an offending or damaging act by another. As you can see from the stages in the growth of law, the typical legal system does not have the attainment of justice as its primary goal. Instead, the goal is to provide a peaceful alternative to individuals who might consider taking personal revenge for the wrongs done to them. This approach is very wise, as justice satisfactory to all parties is almost impossible to achieve in any dispute.

Most court rulings will not even match one party's definition of justice, much less both. Therefore, the legal system must strive to provide a fair and impartial court in which to be heard. Consequently, each party is likely to recognize that he or she has received the best possible result available. This recognition, along with the penalties for taking the law into their own hands, is likely to prevent the losers from taking personal revenge afterwards.

NETBookmark

The legal system in Louisiana—unlike that of any other state—derives from the Civil Code established by French emperor Napoleon in 1804. The other 49 states have systems based on the English common law system. Access www.cengage.com/school/business/21biz and click on the link for Chapter 1. Read the article to learn what makes Louisiana's law unique. Why did Louisiana adopt France's law structure? How does Louisiana's system of "civil law" differ from the "common law" traditions practiced by all the other states?

www.cengage.com/school/business/21biz

How U.S. Law Developed

Although the historical and ethnic backgrounds of the citizens of the United States are diverse, the roots of the vast majority of U.S. laws and legal systems lie in England. There, over the course of centuries, the power to make, interpret, and apply the law was slowly transferred from the monarchy to legal institutions very similar to those of this country.

The system that the King of England set up centuries ago ultimately molded English culture by producing a uniform common law for all of England. This **common law** was based on the customs practiced by most of the realm's people and applicable to all of its subjects. English colonists transported this system of law to this continent. Building on success, the U.S. federal government and all but one of the states have adopted the English common law system as their own.

CheckPOINT

What is the goal of the law?

_____

_____

_____

Law and Ethics

Every society has a unique culture that evolves and changes over time. Each culture develops a set of laws based on the ethical values expressed at the time. Laws evolve as the culture's sense of ethics evolves.

An **ethical system** is a way of deciding what is right or wrong in a consistent, reasoned, impartial manner. Consider the three important elements in this definition.

1. A decision is made about a right or wrong action.

2. The decision is reasoned.

3. The decision is impartial.

TEAMWORK

Work with a partner. Think of a decision that you each made recently that affected another in a significant way. Would you consider that decision to be an ethical decision? Why or why not? Present your findings to the class.

Decision about a Right or Wrong Action

Many of your decisions have little effect on anyone except yourself. For example, your decision to buy blue jeans with wide pant legs instead of narrow ones has no ethical component. On the other hand, your decision to discontinue medical support for an unconscious, terminally ill relative is an intensely ethical decision. To involve ethics, a decision must affect you or others in some significant way.

Reasoned Decisions

You often act in response to your emotions. For example, after watching a movie, you might recommend it to friends with such words as, "It really made me feel good." Or when someone asks you why you made a particular comment, you respond, "I don't really know, I just felt like it." What you mean is that your feelings or emotions guided your actions. To make ethical decisions, you must base your decisions on reason, not on emotion.

People often reason about right and wrong by referring to a time-tested authority. The law is such an authority for some; religious texts are for others. For example, a person might reason, "I believe that following the law in

Why is it important not to base decisions on your emotions?

©Huntstock.com, 2009/Used under license from Shutterstock.com

such a diverse society such as ours is the best solution to any problem because it produces the greatest good for the greatest number."

Impartial Decisions

Impartiality is the idea that the same ethical standards are applied to everyone. If it is wrong for you to engage in a certain action, then in the same circumstance, it is also wrong for me. So, by definition, ethics does not value one person or group of persons more than any other. Each person is an individual and should receive equal respect and consideration from others.

Impartiality requires that, in making ethical decisions, you balance your self-interests with the interests of others. Sometimes it is difficult to recognize the interests of others. Your self-interests can make your perceptions unclear and thus affect your ability to be impartial.

Suppose you lose control of your car while backing out of your driveway. The next thing you know, you have struck and damaged your neighbor's car. You can't decide if you should tell what you did. You might think, "I know my religion teaches me to tell the truth. But it would cost me more than $100 if I admit that I ran into Mrs. Anderson's car. I can't afford that, but she can! So it must be okay to deny my beliefs in this situation. I'm not going to tell her." If you come to this conclusion, you are not being impartial.

Impartiality is especially important when organizations and institutions rather than individuals are involved. When an ethical decision involves an organization, self-interest can make people conclude that their actions will not injure others. "It was only the school's property," or "It doesn't matter, only the insurance company was cheated." In reality, behind all organizations are many people, such as taxpayers, employees, and customers. They are injured when the organization is injured. Property taxes may go up due to school vandalism, or prices in stores may be raised due to shoplifting.

Business Ethics

The reason you are learning about ethics in general is to prepare you to apply ethical concepts to business decision making. *Business ethics* are the ethical principles used in making business decisions. All too often, however, ethics are not considered when business decisions are made. The reason can be summarized in two words: profit maximization.

Those who would move factories offshore or cut jobs and pay in order to reduce costs and produce greater short-term profits support the idea of profit maximization. However, such activities tend to do little more than line the pockets of the business owners. This enriching of the few at the expense of the many occurs because our free-market economy is far from perfect. To achieve a more ethically motivated economy, the profit maximization ethic will need to be replaced by more humane ethical standards.

COMMUNICATE

In the economic downturn of 2008–2009, several large corporations were on the brink of failure, often as a result of the corporation's own poor business practices. Tax dollars were given to these corporations to prevent them from failing and to help restore the economy. Write a one-page argument for and against this practice.

CheckPOINT

What are the three elements in the definition of ethics?

_____

_____

_____

Think Critically

1. What is the difference between law and justice?

_____

_____

_____

_____

2. Why would a ruler (sovereign) be interested in maintaining stability?

_____

_____

_____

_____

3. Why do you think the founding fathers of the United States adopted the English system of common law?

_____

_____

_____

_____

4. Explain the importance of making ethical decisions when dealing with businesses and institutions.

_____

_____

_____

_____

Make Academic Connections

5. **Communication** Using the Internet, research the court systems in England. Present the information you find to your class.

6. **Research** Using the library or Internet, find an alternative to the English system of common law in use today. Create a presentation comparing and contrasting the systems. Discuss some of the differences in class.

7. **Ecology** Make a list of the positive impacts some businesses are having on the environment and natural resources by participating in the green revolution. Choose one of the examples on your list and write a paragraph about how an ethical approach taken by the business resulted in a green solution.

JUMP START

The Erikson Corporation of Springfield, Missouri, is a manufacturer of small trailers useful in transporting boats, riding lawn mowers, and other such items. Erikson ships its trailers on large flatbed trucks to dozens of retailers in neighboring states. Generally, does the U.S. Constitution grant the power to regulate these shipments to the federal government or to the various state governments directly involved?

Sources of Law

In a democracy like the United States, the ultimate lawmaking power is in the hands of the people who are governed by the laws that are made. In the United States, the people have transferred this lawmaking power to federal, state, and local governments. The laws at each level of government consist mainly of constitutions, statutes, administrative regulations, and case law.

Constitutions

A **constitution** is a document that sets forth the framework of a government and its relationship to the people it governs. When constitutions are adopted or amended, or when courts interpret constitutions, *constitutional law* is made. You are governed by both the Constitution of the United States and the constitution of your state. The Supreme Court of the United States is the final interpreter of the federal Constitution. Each state supreme court is the final authority on the meaning of its state constitution.

Constitutions are the highest sources of law, and the federal Constitution is "the supreme law of the land" (U.S. Constitution, Article VI). This means that any federal, state, or local law is not valid if it conflicts with the federal Constitution.

Federal and state constitutions are concerned primarily with defining and allocating certain powers in our society. Constitutions allocate powers between the people and their governments, between state governments and the federal government, and among the branches of the government.

Power, People, and Government The Constitution of the United States of America is the main instrument for allocating powers between the people of this country and their federal government. It does this by granting on behalf of the people certain specified powers to the federal government and by reserving to the people certain rights. This latter function is mostly accomplished through the first ten amendments to the Constitution, called the *Bill of Rights*. Among the personal rights assured by the Bill of Rights are freedom of religion, freedom of speech, and the right to remain silent if accused of a crime. The entire Bill of Rights is shown on the next page.

Comstock Images/Jupiter Images

What is the significance of the Constitution's first three words, "We the People. . ."?

Cross-Cultural Relationships

THE MAGNA CARTA, PETITION OF RIGHT, AND BILL OF RIGHTS

Three English documents provide the basis for our own Bill of Rights. These documents are The Magna Carta, the Petition of Right, and the English Bill of Rights. The Magna Carta is considered the basis for English constitutional liberties. This charter was granted by King John to English barons in 1215. The Magna Carta abolished many abuses and guaranteed certain liberties. The Petition of Right (1628) and the Bill of Rights (1689) reinforced the Magna Carta.

Think Critically

Review the rights protected by your Bill of Rights. Can you think of other important rights that were not mentioned in these original amendments to the U.S. Constitution?

4. Case Law
- creates precedent

U.S. Bill of Rights

The first ten amendments to the Constitution, known as the Bill of Rights, were adopted to ensure that U.S. citizens would enjoy the human rights proclaimed in the Declaration of Independence. The amendments in the Bill of Rights shown below are in the words of our founding fathers.

AMENDMENT I Congress shall make no law respecting an establishment of religion, or prohibiting the free exercise thereof; or abridging the freedom of speech, or of the press, or the right of the people peaceably to assemble, and to petition the Government for a redress of grievances.

AMENDMENT II A well regulated Militia, being necessary to the security of a free State, the right of the people to keep and bear Arms, shall not be infringed.

AMENDMENT III No Soldier shall, in time of peace be quartered in any house, without the consent of the Owner, nor in time of war, but in a manner to be prescribed by law.

AMENDMENT IV The right of the people to be secure in their persons, houses, papers, and effects, against unreasonable searches and seizures, shall not be violated, and no warrants shall issue, but upon probable cause, supported by oath or affirmation, and particularly describing the place to be searched, and the persons or things to be seized.

AMENDMENT V No person shall be held to answer for a capital, or otherwise infamous crime, unless on a presentment or indictment of a Grand Jury, except in cases arising in the land or naval forces, or in the Militia, when in actual service in time of War or public danger; nor shall any person be subject for the same offense to be twice put in jeopardy of life or limb, nor shall be compelled in any criminal case to be a witness against himself, nor be deprived of life, liberty, or property, without due process of law; nor shall private property be taken for public use, without just compensation.

AMENDMENT VI In all criminal prosecutions, the accused shall enjoy the right to a speedy and public trial, by an impartial jury of the State and district wherein the crime shall have been committed, which district shall have been previously ascertained by law, and to be informed of the nature and cause of the accusation; to be confronted with the witnesses against him; to have compulsory process for obtaining witnesses in his favor, and to have the assistance of counsel for his defense.

AMENDMENT VII In Suits at common law, where the value in controversy shall exceed twenty dollars, the right of trial by jury shall be preserved, and no fact tried by a jury, shall be otherwise re-examined in any Court of the United States, than according to the rules of the common law.

AMENDMENT VIII Excessive bail shall not be required, nor excessive fines imposed, nor cruel and unusual punishments inflicted.

AMENDMENT IX The enumeration in the Constitution of certain rights shall not be construed to deny or disparage others retained by the people.

AMENDMENT X The powers not delegated to the United States by the Constitution, nor prohibited by it to the States, are reserved to the States respectively, or to the people.

Power and Federal and State Governments The federal Constitution also allocates powers between the federal and state governments. For example, many governmental powers over business are divided between state governments and the federal government on the basis of commerce. The Constitution gives the federal government the power to regulate both foreign and interstate commerce. Interstate commerce occurs between two or more states.

Power and Branches of Government State and federal constitutions also allocate governmental powers among the executive, legislative, and judicial branches of those governments. Constitutions typically divide such governmental powers among these branches to create a system of checks and balances. These checks and balances ensure that no branch of government becomes so powerful as to dominate the others.

The U.S. Constitution provides an excellent example of the application of the principle of checks and balances. At the federal level, it gives the power to make laws to the *legislative branch*. The power to investigate violations and prosecute alleged violators of these laws is given to the *executive branch*. The power to conduct trials, or formal proceedings that examine and determine legal issues and pronounce judgment, is placed with the *judicial branch*. This separation of powers allows each governmental branch to check or balance out the potential misuse of power by another branch.

Branches of Government	Lawmaking Powers
Legislative	Makes the laws
Executive	Investigates and prosecutes alleged violators
Judicial	Sits in judgment of alleged violators

Statutes

The federal Constitution created the Congress of the United States. State constitutions created the state legislatures. These state and federal legislatures are composed of elected representatives of the people. Acting for their citizens, these legislatures enact laws called **statutes**.

All states delegate some legislative authority to local governments. Thus, towns, cities, and counties can legislate on matters over which the state has given them authority. Such laws are effective only within the boundary of the local governments that enact them. Such legislation is created by a town or city council or by a county board or commission. Legislation at the local level usually is called an *ordinance*.

Administrative Regulations

Federal, state, and local legislatures all create administrative agencies. *Administrative agencies* are governmental bodies formed to carry out particular laws. The federal Social Security Administration, your state's division of motor vehicles, your county's zoning commission, and your city's health department

DID YOU KNOW ?

There are several sources on the Internet where you can learn about current bills being reviewed for passage by your state legislature. You can search for bills by their number or sponsor, read detailed descriptions of them, and check status reports as they move through the legislative process.

Does this sign in a small city represent the result of statutes, ordinances, or administrative regulations?

©Harris Shiffman, 2009/Used under license from Shutterstock.com

are examples of administrative agencies. Although the agencies are created by legislatures, the executive branch of government usually controls administrative agencies. Thus, the President, governor, chief commissioner, or mayor will supervise the agency's activities.

Legislatures sometimes give administrative agencies legislative powers and limited judicial powers. Legislative power means the agency is authorized to create administrative laws also called *rules* and *regulations*. For example, the federal Social Security Administration might set rules for determining *when* a student is a dependent of a widow or widower and qualified to receive social security payments.

If an agency has judicial power, it can hold hearings, make determinations of fact, and apply the law to particular cases. The Social Security Administration might, for example, hold a hearing that decides whether a particular student is in fact a dependent.

The courts have held that the rules and regulations made by agencies have the force of law. Thus, our body of laws is being constantly added to, not only by Congress and the state legislatures, but also by the multitude of state and federal agencies exercising the legislative powers delegated to them. All federal laws, even those made by agencies, are constitutionally supreme when in conflict with state laws.

Case Law

The judicial branch of governments creates case law. Case law usually is made after a trial has ended and one of the parties has appealed to a higher court. This appeal will be based on legal rulings made by the lower court in deciding the case. When the higher or appellate court publishes its opinion on a case, that opinion may state new rules to be used in deciding the case and others like it. These rules are known as **case law**. Federal courts establish federal case law. Similarly, each state creates case law through its state courts.

The effectiveness of case law arises out of the doctrine of *stare decisis*, which is Latin for "to adhere to decided cases." This doctrine requires that lower courts follow established case law in deciding similar cases. The doctrine of *stare decisis* generally does not bind supreme courts. However, even at the supreme court level, established case laws (known as *precedents*) are only changed after in-depth consideration.

CheckPOINT

What are the sources of statutes at each level of government?

_____

_____

_____

Classifications of Laws

Laws may be classified in various ways. Commonly used classifications include civil laws, criminal laws, procedural laws, and substantive laws.

Civil Laws

When the private legal rights of an individual are violated, the matter is governed by civil law. The use of the term civil law within the common law system refers to the group of laws that deal with wrongs against individual persons. Civil law applies whenever one person has a right to sue, or to bring legal action against, another person.

For example, when a tenant fails to pay the rent, the landlord has the right to sue the tenant. The police do not take action in civil conflicts. If a defendant loses a civil case, that defendant is liable. This means that she, he, or it (a business can sue and be sued) must do what the court orders so as to restore the plaintiff to his, her, or its pre-injury state. The payment of money damages is the remedy most often ordered by courts to accomplish this.

Criminal Laws

A *crime* is an offense against society. It disrupts the stable environment that makes civilization work. So, when the citizens' right to live in peace is violated by such activity, the offense is governed by criminal law. Acting in the name of all the people, the government investigates an alleged wrongdoing. If a crime is committed and the person responsible can be found, the government will prosecute. Conviction of a crime can result in a fine, imprisonment, and in some states, execution.

Usually when a crime occurs, private rights of the victim are also violated. A violation may be both a criminal and a civil offense. Thus, the civil law may also apply. The victim of the crime may sue the wrongdoer in addition to bringing criminal charges against the same party.

Procedural Laws

Procedural law deals with methods of enforcing legal rights and duties. Laws that specify how and when police can make arrests and what methods can be used in a trial are procedural laws. Procedural laws determine what remedies are available in a lawsuit. The doctrine of *stare decisis* is a procedural law. Rules for determining the supremacy of conflicting laws are procedural laws.

There are two types of procedural law, civil procedure and criminal procedure. *Criminal procedure* defines the process for enforcing the law when someone is charged with a crime. *Civil procedure* is used when a civil law has been violated. Civil law is concerned only with private offenses. When a civil law is violated, the injured party will follow civil procedure to seek compensation for his or her loss. Police and public prosecutors usually do not get involved in private disputes.

TEAMWORK

In small groups, review different news sources, including the Internet, to find and list examples of at least ten laws. Next to each law on the list, indicate what you think is the source of the law (constitution, statute, administrative regulation, or case law). Discuss your conclusions and the logic behind them as a class.

In 1981, then President Ronald Reagan was shot and wounded by a number of bullets allegedly fired by John Hinckley, a failed songwriter. Hinckley was arrested at the scene literally with the "smoking gun." After criminal proceedings were begun against him, Hinckley was given two different psychiatric exams and found to be competent to stand trial. He subsequently pled not guilty to the charges including the attempted assassination of the President of the United States. Hinckley's attorneys, paid for by his wealthy parents, were able to have critical evidence, in the form of answers given to questions asked by officers before his attorneys were present, thrown out even though he had been read his Miranda rights (which state that he had the right to remain silent, that any statement he made could be used against him in a court of law, that he had the right to the presence of an attorney, and that, if he could not afford an attorney, one would be appointed for him) three times. They were also able to suppress an allegedly incriminating diary discovered in a legitimate search of Hinckley's cell for suicide implements. These denials of evidence to the prosecution for use at trial were based on the Constitutional rights against improper searches and seizures and the right to counsel. As a consequence, Hinckley was found not guilty by reason of insanity and confined to St. Elizabeth's Hospital in Washington, D. C., from which he currently enjoys numerous furloughs each year.

THINK CRITICALLY

Do you think Hinckley's rights were violated in these situations? Are the rights of a defendant absolute over those of the public and the victim regardless of the circumstances? Do you consider the exclusion of evidence the only remedy in such a case? Can you think of other remedies that would be effective in maintaining these constitutional rights?

Substantive Laws

In contrast, *substantive law* defines rights and duties. It is concerned with all rules of conduct, except those involved in enforcement. Substantive laws define offenses, such as murder, theft, vehicular homicide, breach of contract, and negligence.

CheckPOINT

What is the difference between civil and criminal laws and between procedural and substantive laws?

_____

_____

_____

Think Critically

1. Any federal, state, or local law is invalid if it conflicts with the federal Constitution. Explain why this is necessary.

   _____

   _____

2. Which branch of the federal government do you believe is the most powerful today? Why?

   _____

   _____

3. Generally speaking, do you think statutes are clear as to their application and effect when they are drafted? Why or why not?

   _____

   _____

   _____

4. As a future businessperson, do you think you will have more problems with criminal, civil, procedural, or substantive laws? Explain your answer.

   _____

   _____

   _____

Make Academic Connections

5. **Problem Solving** How would you integrate the Internet into the making of laws?

   _____

   _____

   _____

   _____

   _____

6. **History** Using the Internet or library, research the history of the U.S. Constitution. Prepare an oral presentation of your finding for your class.

7. **Social Studies** Contact your local government to find out about ordinances that have recently been enacted. Specifically ask if economic recovery and/or green industry aspects have been considered in the passage of the ordinances. Write a one-page paper describing one of these ordinances and its effect on the citizens of the community.

GOALS

Name the three levels of federal courts

Identify the various types of state and local courts as well as their jurisdictions

KEY TERMS

jurisdiction, p. 19

court of record, p. 22

 JUMP START

The Erikson Corporation, located in Missouri, is owed nearly $65,000 by one of its retailers, Leif and Eric Distributors, located in Kansas. Because the procedural laws of the federal courts are more advantageous, Erikson wants to bring suit in federal court and not in either of the state courts. Given the jurisdictional rules of the federal district courts, can it do so?

The Federal Courts

In the following passage, Article III of the U.S. Constitution gave the power to judge certain criminal and civil matters to a system of federal courts.

> The judicial Power of the United States shall be vested in one supreme Court, and in such inferior Courts as the Congress may from time to time ordain and establish.

The country did not have a Supreme Court under the Articles of Confederation. Some citizens thought that one was not needed under the Constitution. As a result, it wasn't until six months after George Washington's inauguration as our first president that Congress passed the Federal Judiciary Act. This act established the U.S. Supreme Court (USSC) and the circuit courts of appeal. Approximately a century later Congress acted in a similar fashion by creating the federal district courts.

Certain specialized courts, such as those concerned primarily with tax and bankruptcy matters, also have been created as the need for them has arisen. Referring to the figure on the next page will help as you work your way through the following description of the federal judicial system.

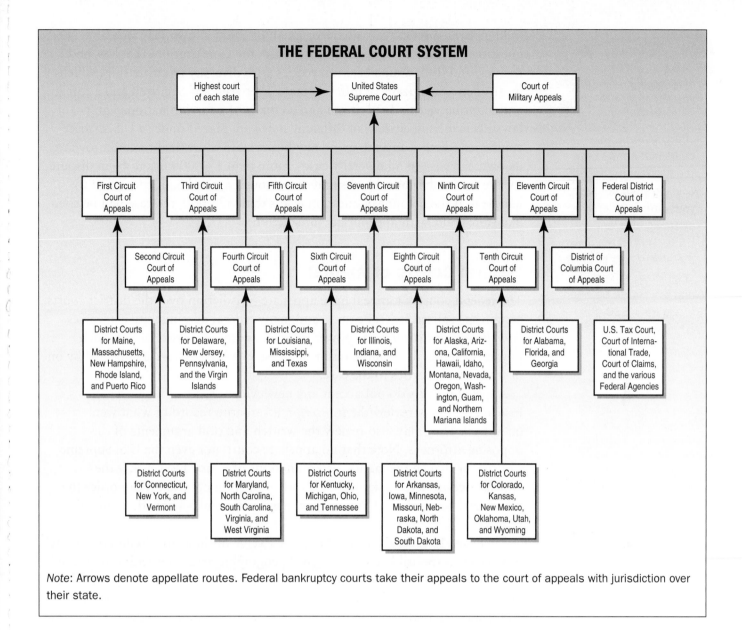

THE FEDERAL COURT SYSTEM

Note: Arrows denote appellate routes. Federal bankruptcy courts take their appeals to the court of appeals with jurisdiction over their state.

Currently there are three levels of federal courts with general jurisdiction—district courts, courts of appeal, and the U.S. Supreme Court. **Jurisdiction** means the power to hear and decide cases. A court with general jurisdiction can hear almost any kind of case. A court with special jurisdiction, such as the U.S. Tax Court, hears only a specific type of case.

U.S. District Courts

At the lowest level of federal courts with general jurisdiction is the U.S. district court. This is the trial court of the federal system. A *trial court* is basically a court in which a case is fully heard for the first time. The power to determine the facts of the matter and to make the initial determination of the law to be used in deciding a case is called *original jurisdiction*. The district courts have that power in the federal system.

In general, district courts have original jurisdiction over (a) "federal questions," which are cases that arise under the Constitution, U.S. law, and U.S. treaties, and (b) lawsuits between parties with diversity of citizenship, which means between citizens of different states, between a U.S. citizen and a foreign nation, or between a U.S. citizen and a citizen of a foreign nation. Significant lawsuits involving citizens of different states are placed under a U.S. district court's jurisdiction so as to avoid any bias a state court might exhibit toward its own citizens. In all diversity cases, more than $75,000 has to be in dispute for the case to be considered significant enough for a U.S. district court to handle it. If the amount in question is less than $75,000, the case will be tried in a state court with appropriate jurisdiction.

Federal Courts of Appeal

The federal courts of appeal have appellate jurisdiction over the district courts, certain specialized federal courts, and many federal administrative agencies. *Appellate jurisdiction* is the power to review cases for errors of law. Such power is exercised when the result of a case in a lower court is appealed by one or more of the parties to the case.

Appellate courts do not accept any new evidence or call witnesses. Instead, they may review the *transcript*, a verbatim record of what went on at trial. They may also review the written and oral arguments of the opposing attorneys. Note that no appellate court, not even the U.S. Supreme Court, can change the factual determinations of a jury. However, if the appellate court detects significant errors in the original trial, it can order that a new trial be conducted. A new jury then would make a new determination of facts.

There are 13 federal courts of appeal. Twelve of these are circuit courts, each of which is responsible for an assigned geographic area. The 13th is dedicated to the "Federal Circuit." As such, it handles patent and claims cases appealed out of the district courts. It also handles appeals from specialized federal courts and from such bodies as the Court of International Trade and the International Trade Commission.

The U.S. Supreme Court

The U.S. Supreme Court (USSC) has both original and appellate jurisdiction. The original jurisdiction of this court is used far less frequently than its appellate jurisdiction. According to the U.S. Constitution, the USSC has original jurisdiction only over cases affecting "Ambassadors, other public Ministers and Consuls, and those in which a State shall be Party."

The appellate jurisdiction of the USSC is exercised over cases on appeal from the U.S. courts of appeal or from the highest courts of the various states. If, after reviewing, the USSC believes that a case contains a constitutional issue that needs to be decided, it will issue a *writ of certiorari* to the last court that heard the case. This "writ," or order, compels the lower court to turn over the record of the case to the Supreme Court for review.

FREEDOM OF SPEECH

In 1996, the U.S. Congress passed the Communications Decency Act (CDA), which attempted to regulate the right to free speech on the Internet. A U.S. district court found the CDA unconstitutional. On appeal in *Reno v. ACLU,* the U.S. Supreme Court held that the CDA's "indecent transmission" and "patently offensive display" provisions inhibited freedom of speech because of their ambiguity. The USSC then declared the provisions as unconstitutional. However, it did leave intact the immunity provisions of the CDA, which protect Internet providers, such as Yahoo, Google, Amazon, eBay and others, from suit due to material created and posted by users. As late as 2009, suits have been brought against the immunity provisions but have failed to alter them significantly.

THINK CRITICALLY

Do you agree or disagree with the government's attempts to regulate free speech on the Internet? Justify your answer.

The USSC's appellate jurisdiction over state supreme court cases is limited to those in which a federal law has been invalidated or whose issues center on the U.S. Constitution. The decisions of the USSC that interpret or apply the U.S. Constitution are final and can only be overturned by the USSC itself or by a constitutional amendment.

CheckPOINT

Over what types of cases do U.S. district courts have original jurisdiction?

_____

_____

_____

State and Local Courts

The typical state legal system mirrors the federal system. The state legislature makes the laws. The state executive branch enforces them before the courts of the state judicial branch. There are state administrative agencies with powers given them by the state legislature. These agencies often complement their counterparts at the federal level. For example, a state Department of Natural Resources is a counterpart to the U.S. Environmental Protection Agency.

State Trial Courts

In most states, the courts with general original jurisdiction over both criminal and civil matters are known as *circuit courts*. In other states, however, they are named superior courts, district courts, or courts of common pleas. Regardless of their title, they are the courts of record of the state system. In a **court of record**, an exact account of what went on at trial is kept so that appeals may be filed. This account may include a transcript of what was said, the evidence that was submitted, statements and determinations of the court officials, and the judgment of the court.

Courts of record will at times review the decisions of, or handle appeals from, courts of inferior jurisdiction. When this occurs, however, they actually retry the cases in full in order to make the proper record in case of appeals. Because it has original jurisdiction over a case before it, a court of record will make determinations of the facts in the case by using a jury or, if a jury is not requested by the appropriate party or parties, by having the presiding judge determine the facts. The court of record will then select and apply the law to the facts to reach a verdict in the case.

State Courts of Appeal

In about half of the states, a panel of no more than three judges from a state court of appeal reviews an appeal of a case in a court of record. In states where this middle level of appellate court does not exist, the appeal goes directly to the highest state court, usually referred to as the state supreme court. The panel from the state court of appeals or supreme court evaluates the record of the case and then hears the attorneys' oral and written arguments. Note that no new evidence can be introduced at this level, so the facts remain unchanged. Basically the appellate judges check to be sure that the correct law was used to resolve the case.

The court of appeals' panel of judges may conclude that the trial court used the wrong law. If so, the panel may enter the correct judgment or send the case back down for a new trial. On the other hand, the judges may conclude the lower court used the correct law in the proper way and, consequently, let the lower court's judgment stand.

State Supreme Courts

In general, a party to a case is entitled to a trial and to one appeal, if the appeal is filed in a timely manner and in the proper form. As mentioned above, a middle-level state court of appeals handles that appeal in about half of the states. Otherwise, the state supreme court handles it.

In states with the middle-level courts of appeal, only cases that involve the most complex legal issues are taken to the justices of the state supreme court. At the state supreme court level, a panel of three or more justices reviews the legal issues and listens to the attorneys' oral arguments.

State supreme courts issue the final decision on matters of law appealed to them unless the U.S. Constitution or other federal issues are involved. In that case, a further appeal can go to the U.S. Supreme Court.

In addition to its appellate jurisdiction, in several states, the state supreme court has original jurisdiction over most state impeachment cases.

DID YOU KNOW ?

Justice is the title given to judges who sit on state supreme courts and the federal Supreme Court.

Impeachment cases involve the trial of governmental officials for misconduct in office. Finally, note that some states name their court of final authority something other than "supreme court." For example, New York calls its highest court the Court of Appeals.

Specialized State Courts

In every state, a number of courts with specialized jurisdiction or jurisdiction inferior to that of the courts of record exist. These courts include the associate circuit, municipal, small claims, juvenile, and probate courts.

Associate Circuit (County) Courts Many states have a layer of courts below their courts of general original jurisdiction. These lower courts are referred to as *associate circuit courts* or *county courts.* Such courts hear minor criminal cases, state traffic offenses, and lawsuits in which relatively small amounts are being disputed, usually no more than $25,000. Generally, these courts are not courts of record. However, they take a significant burden off the higher courts, even though appeals from their decisions can be taken to the circuit courts for a trial on the record.

Municipal Courts Cities typically have courts that administer their ordinances. These *municipal courts* are usually divided into traffic and criminal divisions. As city ordinances often overlap or duplicate state laws, less serious violations that occur within city limits end up before such municipal courts for their first trial. The result can then be appealed to the circuit court level if necessary.

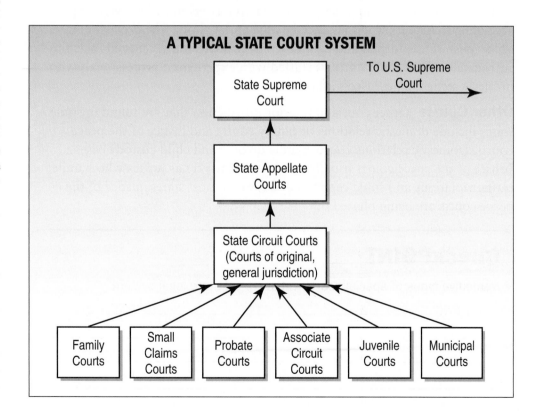

A TYPICAL STATE COURT SYSTEM

To U.S. Supreme Court

State Supreme Court

State Appellate Courts

State Circuit Courts (Courts of original, general jurisdiction)

Family Courts · Small Claims Courts · Probate Courts · Associate Circuit Courts · Juvenile Courts · Municipal Courts

Small Claims Courts Many relatively minor individual suits would not be heard if not for the small claims courts. These courts handle cases in which small amounts, typically $2,500 or less, are concerned. The cases are handled informally before a judge and without a jury. The costs of filing such cases are held to a minimum. Attorneys often are not allowed or are allowed only if they're acting for themselves or for a corporation of which they are salaried employees. The decisions of a small claims court can be appealed to the circuit court level.

Juvenile Courts Individuals under the age of full responsibility for their criminal acts, generally 18 years, are known as *juveniles*. To protect such individuals from the full consequences of their criminal acts, special courts have been set up. These courts ensure that most of the criminal cases involving juveniles do not become public knowledge. The courtroom is closed while an informal hearing into the charges is conducted. Any records made are not open to the public.

The juvenile is entitled to his or her full constitutional rights, including the right of representation by an attorney. Should the juvenile be judged guilty of the charges, the court has wide powers in determining what should be done for rehabilitation. Possibilities open to the court include release into the supervision of parents, guardians, or governmental officials. Alternatives include placing juveniles in foster homes or correctional facilities.

Most states also provide that a juvenile of at least 16 years of age can be tried and punished as an adult in cases in which the juvenile allegedly committed murder or other very serious offense. Appeals from actions of the juvenile courts are directed to the circuit courts.

Probate Courts A probate court is charged with handling wills and estates. When an individual dies, the deceased's assets must be divided up according to his or her wishes and the appropriate laws. The procedure to accomplish this is formal and complex. The probate court, referred to as the surrogate court in some states, is staffed with experienced professionals who properly settle the deceased's affairs.

Other Courts Other courts of inferior jurisdiction that are found in some states include domestic relations or family courts and justice of the peace courts. Domestic relations courts handle divorce and child custody cases. Justice of the peace courts usually employ nonlawyers as judges who handle traffic violations and some ceremonial duties. In most states, justice of the peace courts are being phased out.

CheckPOINT

Name five types of special courts in the typical state legal system.

_____

_____

_____

Think Critically

1. In order for a U.S. district court to handle a case between parties with diversity of citizenship, the amount in dispute must be more than $75,000. Why is such a high figure necessary?

Specialized courts hear cases that fall under their special narrowly focused jurisdiction.

For example, there are mental health

_____

_____

_____

2. Judging from the chart of the federal court system on page 19, what do you think of the workload of the U.S. Supreme Court?

_____

_____

_____

_____

_____

3. Why are the appeals of the federal agencies not routed to the U.S. district courts instead of the federal courts of appeals?

_____

_____

_____

_____

4. Why are the records of juvenile offenders kept closed?

_____

_____

_____

_____

Make Academic Connections

5. **Research** Interview available judges on various courts. Ask them to evaluate their job and position, and what they would change, among other questions. Write a one-page report of your findings.

6. **Geography** On a U.S. map, draw and then evaluate the jurisdictional boundaries of the various federal and state courts. Write a paragraph explaining why you think the boundaries were established this way.

ASSESSMENT

Chapter Summary

1.1 **Law, Justice, and Ethics**

   A. Legal systems are created to provide social stability by allowing individuals access to an impartial way to resolve disputes.

   B. An ethical decision is about choosing between a right or wrong action and is reached through a consistent, reasoned, impartial process.

1.2 **Types of U.S. Law**

   A. The primary source of power for a democracy is the consent of the people. Typically in a democracy, this consent is expressed most directly by the adoption of a constitutional framework for the government.

   B. Laws may be classified in many ways—as statutory vs. case law, criminal vs. civil law, substantive vs. procedural law, and federal vs. state law.

1.3 **Federal and State Legal Systems**

   A. U.S. district courts, federal courts of appeal, and the United States Supreme Court are the main courts in the federal system.

   B. State circuit courts, state courts of appeal, and a state supreme court are the principal courts in most state systems.

Vocabulary Builder

Choose the term that best fits the definition. Write the letter of the answer in the space provided. Some terms may not be used.

_____ 1. The power to hear and decide cases

_____ 2. Laws created by state and federal legislatures

_____ 3. A court in which an exact account of what went on in a trial is kept so as to allow appeals

_____ 4. Laws that regulate the establishment, operation, and termination of commercial enterprises

_____ 5. Rules of conduct that a political authority will enforce

_____ 6. A group of laws within the common law that deals with the wrongs against individual persons

_____ 7. Law based on the customs of the people

_____ 8. A way of deciding what is right or wrong in a reasoned, impartial manner

_____ 9. A document that sets forth the framework of a government and its relationship to the people it governs

_____ 10. Law created by the judicial branch of government that states new rules to be used in deciding a case and subsequent cases like it

a. business law

b. case law

c. civil law

d. common law

e. constitution

f. court of record

g. criminal law

h. ethical system

i. jurisdiction

j. laws

k. statutes

Review Concepts

Point Your
Browser
www.cengage.com/
school/business/21biz

11. What are the stages in the growth of law?

_____

_____

_____

12. Explain the conflict between business ethics and profit maximization.

_____

_____

_____

_____

13. What is the difference between criminal and civil laws, between procedural and substantive laws, between state and federal laws, and between statutory and case law?

_____

_____

_____

_____

_____

14. What are the two jurisdictional bases of the U.S. district courts?

_____

_____

15. What is the significance of a court of record?

_____

_____

16. What is the jurisdiction of a typical municipal court?

_____

_____

17. How are small claims courts different from other courts with original jurisdiction?

_____

_____

18. How are juveniles handled by the court system?

_____

_____

_____

_____

Apply What You Learned

19. Do religions provide you with ethical systems? Explain your answer.

_____

_____

_____

20. What would you envision as a fifth stage in the growth of law?

_____

_____

_____

21. Bennie Tompkins is 10 years old. At the urging of his parents, he auditions for a role in a movie about a child accidentally left behind in a large retail establishment. The movie is a hit, and there will doubtlessly be a sequel that will pay Bennie several million dollars more than the $500,000 he received for the current flick. By law in the state where he resides, Bennie's pay is turned over to his parents. They immediately use it to buy a new house, car, beach home, and various other expensive items. Bennie feels that his parents should be saving some money for his future, such as for his college education. When he asks them to do so, they refuse and point out that until he enters his majority, what he makes is theirs by law. Which source—the judicial or the legislative branch of government—do you feel would be most likely to provide a practical solution to Bennie's legal problem? Why?

_____

_____

_____

_____

22. Why are fines that are imposed as punishments for criminal acts typically paid to the government and not to the victims of the crimes?

_____

_____

_____

23. With which court system, the state or the federal, are you most likely to have firsthand experience? Why?

_____

_____

24. Why do civil cases with large amounts in dispute and involving citizens of different states come under the jurisdiction of the federal courts?

_____

_____

_____

Make Academic Connections

25. **Environment** Profit maximization often conflicts with ethical treatment of the environment. What federal agency is responsible for protecting the environment? What laws does it enforce?

_____

_____

_____

_____

26. **Marketing** Read through several magazines and/or newspapers noting the advertisements of law firms. What types of services do these firms offer? Why do you think these services are offered and not others? Make a spreadsheet of your results.

27. **Communication** The Bill of Rights guarantees individuals certain freedoms. Write a one- or two-page report detailing which of these rights affects businesses and how.

28. **Research** If you had a question involving a state law, a city ordinance, or a bill up for consideration by the legislature, could you look up these items on the Internet? Surf the Internet to find websites where you can access the federal, state, and city law codes and items before the legislature. Make a list of the websites you find and share it in class.

_____

_____

_____

Ethical Dilemma

29. Dry Run Cleaners, Inc., has always employed 20 plus people in its cleaning process. However, the process generates several gallons of liquid toxic residue a week as well as fumes that are a mild health hazard for nearby residents. Recently, a new green machine that is totally self-contained and that releases only a small amount of nontoxic powder each month has come on the market. In addition, its automated system would cut the Dry Run Cleaners' workforce to four employees. Over half of the current workforce have been with the company for many years and are nearing retirement. Given recent setbacks in the local economy, most of them would have to sell their homes and move away to find other employment. Evaluate the moral and ethical questions facing the management of Dry Run Cleaners. What would you recommend the company do?

_____

_____

_____

_____

Law of Contracts

Careers in Business Law

CISCO SYSTEMS INC.

Cisco Systems Inc. is the worldwide leader in providing management systems and networking equipment for the Internet. Employing nearly 65,000 workers with revenues of almost $40 billion, the company serves businesses that maintain their own networks as well as companies that provide information services to others. Cisco relies heavily on the skill and expertise of those who set down the framework for its various business deals in the form of contracts.

Contract Negotiators at Cisco Systems need a thorough understanding of the law of contracts. They must have strong negotiation skills and be able to clearly communicate contract issues with Cisco's top manager, legal counselors, customers, and suppliers. The position requires a bachelor's degree in Business or Marketing and five or more years of experience negotiating technology-related contracts.

Think Critically

1. Why do Contract Negotiators at Cisco Systems need strong communication skills?
2. Do you think contracts for technology-related products differ much from those for other types of products? Why?

PROJECT | Contracts In Your Life

Project Objectives

- Recognize the importance of contracts in your life
- Understand how contracts are made

Getting Started

Read the Project Process below. Make a list of any materials you will need.

- Keep a diary for a week of all the agreements you observed being made either by yourself or others.
- Note which agreements produced the desired results.

Project Process

2.1 Review the agreements you made. Which are express, implied, or quasi contracts? Which are valid, voidable, or void? Which are bilateral or unilateral? Which are executed or remain executory? Remember, it is possible to have an express, valid, bilateral, executed contract.

2.2 Identify the elements of each contract. Who placed each contract in its final form? What were its terms? How was it accepted? What was the consideration?

2.3 Evaluate the parties to the contract and their ability to understand it. Do they have the capacity to contract? If not, why not? Was their assent genuine? If not, what facts call it into question?

2.4 Review the form and nature of the contract. Should it have been in writing? Is each contract within the boundaries of legality and public policy?

Chapter Review

Project Wrap-up Prepare a chart that contrasts the number of agreements with the number of legally enforceable contracts. Note the number and categories of the agreements or contracts that are not enforceable in a court of law and why.

GOALS

Name the six essential elements of a legally enforceable contract

Identify ways to classify contracts

KEY TERMS

contract, p. 32

express contract, p. 33

implied contract, p. 33

valid contract, p. 34

offer, p. 35

 JUMP START

Almost every lunch hour, Chase quickly made three tacos from the make-your-own taco bar at Jose's Taqueria. Jose always had a joke to pass on while he rang up the transaction. Chase would then buy a soda out of the machine, grab a section of the paper the restaurant provided, and settle into one of the booths to read. Chase only had 30 minutes for lunch, so he made the most of them. One day he found the restaurant packed with high school students on their way to a state basketball playoff game. The bus had stopped for them to buy lunch. Twelve students were waiting in line at the register. Seeing his lunchtime evaporating, Chase held up his tacos where Jose could see them and laid the customary amount on the back counter. Jose nodded, winked, and grabbed the money for the register. What kind of contract had just been formed?

Photodisc/Getty Images

What Is a Contract?

A **contract** is an agreement between two or more parties that creates an obligation of some type. The resulting obligation may be legally enforceable or merely a moral obligation which cannot be pursued in a court of law. The framers of the Constitution guaranteed the freedom to make agreements in Article I, Section 10. The states also are ordered not to "pass any. . . Law impairing the Obligation of Contracts." The freedom to contract, however, is not without legal bounds. For example, note that the ban against interfering with the obligation of contracts is not directed at the federal government, but at the states.

There are many situations in which courts will not enforce contracts. Certainly if a person can't get such help from the legal system, the risk of loss in contracting goes way up. Thus, the ability to determine which contracts can be enforced in court and which contracts cannot is very important.

Contracts have six elements essential to their being enforceable in court. A court must find these elements before it will conclude that one or all of the parties to a contract are bound to carry out the contract's terms. The essential elements of a legally enforceable contract are listed below.

1. agreement comprised of an offer and an acceptance

2. supported by consideration

3. made by parties with capacity to contract

4. genuinely assented to

5. for a legal purpose

6. in writing when required

TEAMWORK

Work as a team to compile a list of the contracts in which team members have entered. Which of these contracts would you want to avoid in the future? Be prepared to discuss and justify your choices to the rest of the class.

CheckPOINT

What are the six elements of a legally enforceable contract?

_____

_____

_____

Terms for Understanding Contracts

Contracts can be categorized in many ways. Contracts may be express, implied, or quasi. They may be valid, voidable, or void. They may be executed or executory. And they may be unilateral or bilateral. Note that the use of a term from one grouping does not preclude the use of a term from each of the other groups. For instance, it is possible to have an express, valid, executed, bilateral contract.

Express, Implied, and Quasi Contracts

One of the most important ways to categorize contracts is to look at how clearly their terms are stated. For example, an **express contract** has its terms set down in a clear-cut fashion, either orally or in writing. An oral contract generally is just as binding as a written one. However, the terms of a written contract are usually much easier to prove. Unlike an express contract, the terms of an **implied contract** are not stated. Instead, they are determined from the surrounding circumstances or an established pattern of dealings.

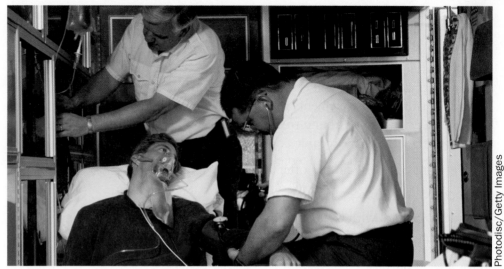

Why might a quasi contract be applied to a medical emergency?

A *quasi contract*, also referred to as an *implied-at-law contract*, exists only by the direction of the court. It does not stem from the agreement of the parties to it. A quasi contract is best viewed as a remedy that the courts utilize to return value to someone who has enriched another person in the absence of an express or implied contract between them. Typically, the price in such a contract will be set at a "reasonable amount" by a jury or judge. Consider the following example.

Basil swerved and hit the brakes as soon as he saw the front tire of the kid's bike peek out from behind the parked car. The brakes locked. His 18-wheeler skidded sideways across the opposite lane and into a guardrail. The impact snapped Basil's head into the door window. He opened the door of the cab and staggered out. A man in a postal uniform ran up to him. Basil stammered, "Is the kid all right?" "Sure," came the man's reply. "Good job. The kid's fine, but you're not." Basil realized he was losing consciousness. "Please don't send me to a hospital...I can't afford it...," Basil said as he slumped to the ground. An ambulance arrived and rushed him to St. John's Medical Center. When he awoke in a hospital bed, he tried to leave and refused to pay. Regardless, a court would find that a quasi contract existed and would force payment of a reasonable value to the hospital for its services. Otherwise, Basil would be unjustly enriched.

Valid, Voidable, and Void Contracts

Another set of terms useful in describing contracts is *valid*, *voidable*, and *void*. A **valid contract** is one that is legally binding and enforceable. In the event of a problem, any party to a valid contract can take it to court for enforcement.

A *voidable contract* is a contract that is initially considered valid but whose legal effect can be cancelled by one or more of the parties to it. This power to cancel or *avoid* a contract is given by law to individuals whose ability to enter into binding agreements is in question. Contracts made by minors, for example, are voidable until sometime after they enter their legal adulthood, usually

CYBERCONTRACTING

By a federal law passed in the year 2000, electronic signatures and contracting—such as those given or entered into over the Internet—were made as binding as though on paper. Given the level of criminal activity by hackers and identity thieves on the Internet, the safety of such electronic commitments has been called into question.

THINK CRITICALLY

Research the safeguards that are available to protect the consumer in electronic transactions. Would you be willing to enter into a cybercontract? Why or why not?

age 18 for contracts. When a minor uses his or her right to avoid, the contract is *rescinded*. This means not only that any current or future effect of the contract is cancelled, but also that the minor is restored as much as possible to her or his previous position. If the power to avoid is not utilized, the contract is considered valid and enforced as such.

Finally, a *void contract* is one that has no legal effect whatsoever. Generally, the courts will not even recognize its existence. Gambling and bribery agreements are typical examples of contracts that courts will not enforce.

Executed and Executory Contracts

An *executed contract* is one that all parties have fully performed. On the other hand, a contract in which some performance has yet to be delivered is termed an *executory contract*. When a dispute about a contract arises, the types of remedies available in a court of law depend on whether the contract is executed or executory.

Unilateral and Bilateral Contracts

Technically, a *bilateral contract* is one that obligates all parties to it to perform according to their promises. A *unilateral contract*, on the other hand, is a contract in which one party is only obligated to fulfill a contractual promise if another party first performs a particular act.

To better understand how these terms are applied, we need to define some other contractual terms. To begin with, an **offer** is a proposal of a bargain or exchange to another party or parties. The person making the offer is termed the *offeror*. The person to whom it is made is termed the *offeree*. For example, if you proposed to sell your laptop computer for $1,200 to your friend Dave, you would be the offeror and Dave the offeree in relation to that offer. Assume that you and Dave haggle for a while. Finally, Dave counteroffers $1,000, and you agree. Regarding the counteroffer, Dave is the offeror and you are the offeree. You and Dave thereby form a contract that calls for Dave to buy the computer

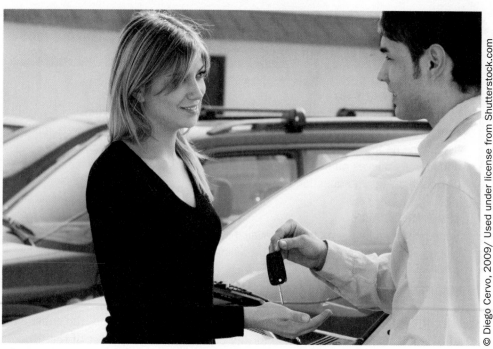

If you offer to sell your car to a friend and she accepts, what promises have been made?

for that amount. That contract involves two promises to which you and Dave may be legally bound. You promise to transfer ownership of the computer to Dave. Dave promises to pay you $1,000 at the time you do so.

In relation to your promise to transfer ownership, you are the maker of that promise, or the *promisor*. Dave is the person to whom the promise is made, or the *promisee*. In relation to Dave's promise to pay, he is the promisor and you are the promisee. Finally, your exchange of promises to each other creates obligations to fulfill those promises. You are the *obligor* who must fulfill your obligation to transfer ownership. Dave is the person to whom you are obliged, or the *obligee*. In like manner, Dave is the obligor in relation to his promise to pay $1,000 in cash for the computer. You are the obligee of that obligation.

In short, both of you are mutually obligated, one to another, to fulfill your contract. When a contract includes such mutual obligations, the law terms it a bilateral contract.

Unilateral contracts, on the other hand, are most often found in reward situations. You offer to pay $25 to anyone who returns the wallet you lost. Does your offer obligate anyone to perform the act? Not at all. But if anyone does perform that act, you are obligated to pay that person the $25.

CheckPOINT

What are the different categories of contracts?

_____

_____

_____

Think Critically

1. How important is the ability to enter into a legally enforceable contract to your everyday life? Could you exist without it? Why or why not?

_____

_____

_____

2. Instead of a contractually based system where each person identifies and provides for the satisfaction of his or her needs, would a command (planned) economic system where each person is told what to produce and consume work better? Why or why not?

_____

_____

_____

3. Give an example of why someone might want to avoid a contract.

_____

_____

4. Why would different remedies for breach of contract be available depending upon whether or not a contract is executed or merely executory?

_____

_____

_____

_____

_____

Make Academic Connections

5. **Research** Evaluate how easy it is to enter into contracts on the Internet for food, clothing, shelter, and other essentials of life. Write a paragraph describing your experience.

6. **History** The feudal period in Europe did not have the level of trade and commerce that is part of our lives today. Read about the quality of life during this period. What were the pros and cons of living at that time?

7. **Geography** On a world map, identify the countries that still embrace the concept of a command economy, where individuals do not have the ability to contract for their own needs and wants.

GOALS

Explain how to create a valid offer

Describe the various ways an offer can be terminated before acceptance

Recognize the importance of acceptance and consideration to contract formation

KEY TERMS

acceptance, p. 42

consideration, p. 43

 JUMP START

Bill and Miko agree to go to the movies together. Miko buys a new outfit for the occasion. Bill buys two tickets. If either party attempts to back out, can the courts be used to enforce their social agreement or to provide a damage award for their lost investments? Why or why not?

Photodisc/Getty Images

The Offer

An *offer* is a proposal of a bargain or exchange to another party or parties. If the offeree accepts the proposal, a contract arises. Generally, to create a valid offer the following must occur.

1. The offeror must intend to create a legal obligation as judged from the standpoint of a reasonable observer

2. The terms must be complete and definite

3. The offer must be communicated to the offeree

Intent to Create a Legal Obligation

The law will only recognize that an offer exists when the offeror seemingly intends to create a legal obligation from the standpoint of a reasonable observer.

Test of the Reasonable Observer When the law must determine if the offeror intended to make the offer in question, the focus is not on what was actually in the mind of the person making the offer. Rather, it is concerned with how the alleged offeror's actions would be interpreted by a reasonable observer. If you are joking when you offer your neighbor twice the value of a car she has for sale, but a reasonable person would interpret your conduct as an indication that you intend to contract, the law will hold that you have actually made such an offer. On the other hand, if you are serious, but a reasonable person would interpret your conduct as a joke, then no offer has been made from a legal standpoint. This is called the *test of the reasonable person*. It is an objective legal test rather than a subjective test based on what you say you were thinking. Businesses and the law need a consistent way to determine when an offer is made. A subjective test would let people escape contractual responsibilities by lying about what they were thinking.

Note that some agreements are unenforceable even if a reasonable person would conclude that they were made. For example, social agreements such as dates do not produce legally enforceable contracts. In the case of Bill and Miko, the courts could not be used to force either party to fulfill the agreement to go to the movie or to pay damages for harm caused by not doing so.

Invitations to Negotiate Most advertisements in newspapers and magazines, on radio or television, or in direct mailings usually are not offers. Instead, courts treat them as invitations to make offers. This allows the would-be seller to test the market and adjust the price accordingly. If you placed a classified ad in the newspaper to sell your riding lawnmower for $350 and 10 people promptly called and said they were driving over with cash in their hands, you would probably adjust the price upward. The law allows this.

Even so, advertisements occasionally may be offers. For example, an ad may become an offer if it asks the offeree to perform an act as a way of accepting. An ad that states that a clearly described new 160-piece tool set will be sold for $20 "to the first person to appear at the front door of our hardware store on Saturday morning after 6:00 A.M." would be a valid offer.

Offer Must Be Complete and Definite

The terms of an offer must be complete and clear enough to allow a court to determine what the parties intended and identify the parties' legal rights and duties.

Complete If an offer is missing essential information, it is incomplete and legally ineffective. Nearly all offers must identify the price, subject matter, and quantity, either directly or indirectly. The amount of essential information to include depends upon the complexity of the transaction. For example, in most states the essential terms for the sale of real estate lots would include

1. identity of the specific lot
2. price
3. full terms for payment
4. date for delivery of possession
5. date for delivery of the deed

COMMUNICATE

Write an advertisement that can be considered an offer. Make up the details of the product and offer. Present the ad in class and explain why it is an offer.

If one of those terms is missing, there is not a valid offer. In contrast, an offer for the sale of a candy bar by the local market typically identifies price, subject matter, and quantity—as many as are on the shelf.

Definite Each essential term must be identified clearly in order for the courts to enforce an agreement. In the sale of real estate lots, for example, a specific lot must be identified. In some contracts, however, a term might be implied by law or common business practice. For example, in contracts between merchants for the sale of goods, when the price is not specified, current market price is the basis for the contract.

Offer Must Be Communicated to the Offeree

A person who is not the intended offeree cannot accept the offer. Nor can a person accept an offer without knowing it has been made. That is because any action taken would not have been a response to the offer. Thus, an offer of a reward that is made to certain persons or even to the general public cannot be accepted by someone who has never seen or heard of the offer. In such cases, the offeror may get what was sought, but most courts require that anyone who claims the reward must have known of the offer and acted in response to it.

CheckPOINT

What are the three conditions for an offer to be valid?

_____

_____

_____

Possible Termination of the Offer before Acceptance

Even if a valid offer is made, it will not be available for acceptance forever. Many different events and circumstances can terminate it.

Revocation

Generally, anytime before an offer has been accepted by the offeree, the offeror may withdraw or *revoke* it. This revocation must be communicated to the offeree to be effective.

Expiration of a Set Period or a Reasonable Time

If there is a time set in the offer for it to remain open, it will expire at the end of that period. Note that the offeror may revoke it even before the set time elapses, however. (The offeree may bind the offeror to holding the offer open for the set period by paying the offeree to do so. This is called buying an *option*.) When nothing is said in the offer about the length of its life, it is alive for a reasonable length of time. What is reasonable depends on the surrounding circumstances.

For example, a produce broker in New Jersey telephones a customer in upper Michigan offering to sell a truckload of tomatoes. If the offer to sell the tomatoes is not accepted within a few hours, it probably will terminate automatically. That is because tomatoes are perishable produce that must be marketed and shipped quickly. The seller may be in touch with many prospective buyers, and they all understand they must accept quickly.

In contrast, an offer to sell expensive durable equipment, such as a truck and trailer, would not terminate until a longer time had elapsed. At least several days would probably be reasonable. If the parties had bargained about the sale over a period of months, a week or longer might be appropriate. To avoid misunderstandings, it is best to specify the time available for acceptance.

Digital Vision/Getty Images

Why is it best to set an expiration date on an offer?

Rejection by the Offeree

An offer clearly rejected by the offeree is terminated. For example, John told Frances that she could buy his car "anytime in the next two weeks for $7,800." Upon hearing the offer, she immediately told John that she didn't want his "old rattletrap" at any price. Almost immediately after she had said it, she remembered that her friend Marcie had mentioned that she wanted a car exactly like it and would pay $12,000. Frances quickly said, "Wait. I accept your offer. I'll pay the $7,800." John, insulted by her original response, refused to agree. When she took him to court to force the sale, the court stated that John's offer was terminated when she refused it, even though he had offered her two weeks to accept it. The entire offer was terminated by her rejection.

Counteroffers

A counteroffer is treated in exactly the same way as a rejection of the original offer. A *counteroffer* occurs if the offeree changes the terms of the offer in any significant way. In the example with John and Frances, if Frances had made a counteroffer of a different monetary amount, say $6,000, John's original offer would have been immediately terminated just as with her outright rejection. Note that if Frances had bought an option to purchase the car for $7,800 anytime during the next two weeks, neither her rejection nor her counteroffer would have cancelled it.

Other Circumstances

Death or insanity of either the offeror or the offeree before acceptance terminates the offer. The destruction of the specific subject matter also terminates an offer. If John's car were in a wreck and destroyed before Frances could accept the offer, the offer would be considered terminated by a court and no contract could result.

CheckPOINT

What events and circumstances can terminate an offer?

_____

_____

_____

Acceptance and Consideration

In addition to the offer, the elements of a legally enforceable contract involve acceptance of the offer, supported by consideration.

Acceptance

An **acceptance** is the agreement by an offeree to the terms of the offer. Acceptances must be absolute and unconditional, otherwise they will be treated by the courts as counteroffers. Note that only offerees

Why is acceptance an important part of the contract process?

Photodisc/Getty Images

can accept, and the acceptance must be communicated to the offeror in order to be legally effective. The silence of the offeree will not be treated as acceptance. Also, if a method of acceptance is specified by the offeror in the offer, it must be followed or the acceptance will not be valid.

It may become important to determine even more precisely when acceptance is effective. Oral acceptances are effective at the moment the words are spoken to the offeror. Acceptances sent by mail usually take effect when properly posted, that is, placed with correct address and sufficient postage under the control of the U.S. Postal Service. A fax acceptance is instantaneous when the transmission lines are open and both sending and receiving equipment work properly. The effect is similar to oral acceptance, but in a more durable form that is easier to prove in court.

The offeror may specify that an acceptance will not be binding until it is actually received. This avoids the confusion that arises when an acceptance is mailed or faxed yet never reaches the offeror.

Consideration

Consideration is what the offeror demands, and generally must receive, in order to make the offer legally enforceable against the offeror. The main purpose of the doctrine of consideration is to distinguish between a stated intent to make a gift, which is generally unenforceable, and the contractual promises that the law must enforce.

There are three requirements of consideration.

1. It must at least entail the making of a promise, performance of an act, or a forbearance from acting.

2. Each party's consideration must be in exchange for consideration given by the other party.

3. What each party exchanges must have legal value; that is, it must be worth something in the eyes of the law.

NETBookmark

In 2007, baseball player Alex Rodriguez set a record for the most lucrative sports contract in history when he signed a $275 million, ten-year agreement with the New York Yankees. Access www.cengage.com/school/business/21biz and click on the link for Chapter 2. Read the story about Rodriguez and his record-setting deal, then answer: Who are the obligors and obligees under this contract? What is the consideration Rodriguez is to receive? What is the consideration the Yankees are to receive?

www.cengage.com/school/business/21biz

CheckPOINT

Define acceptance and consideration.

_____

_____

_____

Think Critically

1. Do you think it is a good idea to evaluate contractual offers objectively? Why or why not?

2. Why isn't an invitation to negotiate treated as an offer?

3. Why do you think offers are terminated on the death of either the offeror or the offeree?

4. How does the law treat a would-be acceptance that does not exactly match the offer?

Make Academic Connections

5. **Ecology** Could you pass a law specifying that every contract have a term in it requiring that all parties to it not hurt the environment in any way? Would such a law be a good idea? Why or why not?

6. **Marketing** Go through your local newspaper and select at least two ads that are invitations to negotiate yet still enforceable against their maker due to their terms. Write a sentence that explains the reasons you think the ads are enforceable. Share your ads and explanations in small groups.

JUMP START

Yakov, age 16, was shopping at a large electronics store when a 3D high-definition, flat screen television caught his eye. A salesman noticed him admiring the TV and persuaded him to buy it. Yakov's aunt had recently died, leaving him a large sum of money for college. Yakov knew the inheritance would pay for the TV, with money left over for the necessary cables and a new 3D high-definition DVD player. A week after making the purchase, however, Yakov realized that he had made a tremendous mistake. Can he return the TV, DVD player, and other accessories and get his money back? Why or why not?

GOALS

Determine if someone has the capacity to contract

Identify when apparent assent to a contract is not genuine

KEY TERMS

necessaries, p. 46
ratification, p. 46
misrepresentation, p. 48
fraud, p. 48

Digital Vision/Getty Images

Capacity to Contract

Once an agreement is formed and supported by consideration, the basics of an enforceable contract have been created. Of the six essential elements of a contract, the requirements of having capacity, genuineness of assent, a legal purpose, and the proper form are important only from the standpoint that they may prove this basic agreement unenforceable.

When one or more of these four elements are not present, the law may allow a party to back out of an otherwise binding contract. One such instance involves individuals who lack the basic ability to properly evaluate and control their entry into contracts. In other words, they lack what the law refers to as *contractual capacity*. The law defines this as the ability to understand the consequences of a contract. This is not a demanding requirement. The law does not require the actual understanding, just "the ability to understand."

Also, this ability to understand does not apply to the contract itself, but to "the consequences of the contract." The "consequences" will satisfy the law if, financial and otherwise, they are generally capable of being expressed in common-sense terms. Three instances in which the law recognizes a lack of contractual capacity are for minors, the insane, and the intoxicated.

Minors

Under criminal and civil law, children under the age of seven cannot be held responsible for a crime or a personal injury they inflict. Contract law grants a somewhat similar status for individuals who enter into contracts while under a certain specified legal age. These individuals are referred to as minors. In most states, this age is set at 18.

Do you think minors should be held responsible when they enter into a contract? Why or why not?

There are two basic protections granted to minors and others who lack capacity. When protected parties purchase **necessaries**—things needed to maintain life and lifestyle, such as food, clothing, and shelter—they need pay only the fair market value rather than the contracted price. When protected parties purchase unnecessary items, they must pay the contracted price but retain the legal ability to avoid (disaffirm) the contract. When a party disaffirms a contract, that party indicates a refusal to be bound by it.

Minors may disaffirm contracts for nonnecessaries during their minority. In addition, minors will be given a reasonable period of time after they reach their contractual majority to determine which contracts they wish to disaffirm. However, the power to disaffirm is immediately cut off if the person ratifies the contract after reaching the age of majority. **Ratification** occurs when a person acts toward the contract as though he or she intends to be bound by it. Ratification cannot occur before the age of majority regardless of what the minor does to affirm the obligation. If the minor properly and in a timely fashion disaffirms the contract, he or she is entitled to receive all the consideration paid into the transaction.

Mental Incapacity

Mental incapacity is much less precisely defined than minority. The test to determine such incapacity is whether the party understands the consequences of his or her contractual acts. People with severe mental illness, severe mental retardation, or severe senility lack capacity.

TEAMWORK

Work in teams to compile a list of necessaries and nonnecessaries in daily life. As a class, compare the lists and debate the differences. Then vote on each item named and compile a final list for each category.

If a judge rules that a person is permanently insane, then the law holds that the person has a complete lack of capacity. As a consequence, all contracts executed by this person are void, whether for necessaries or nonnecessaries. The court will then appoint a *guardian*, who is charged with the responsibility of managing the insane party's property for the good of that party. Note, however, that the insane party's obligations for the fair market value of necessaries must be paid. A person may also be held to have been temporarily insane by the court. In such a case, any contracts made by the person during the period of temporary insanity are considered to be capable of being disaffirmed or ratified as soon as the person becomes *lucid* (clearheaded).

DID YOU KNOW ?

If a person who has been held to be permanently insane or a habitual drunkard writes you a check, the check is void.

Intoxication

Intoxication can arise from using alcohol such as beer or vodka, from using drugs such as marijuana or LSD, or inhaling products such as glue or aerosols. Many courts, however, are reluctant to allow disaffirmance for temporary intoxication when it may injure another. These courts will do so only for those who were so intoxicated that they did not know they were contracting. This stricter standard is used because intoxication is a voluntary act. If a court is called upon to determine if a party is a *habitual drunkard*, that is, a party who cannot turn down a drink when offered, the same rules apply as are applied to the permanently insane.

CheckPOINT

What are the three most notable instances in which the law generally recognizes a lack of contractual capacity?

_____

_____

_____

Lack of Genuine Assent

Another instance in which individuals may be released from contractual obligations is when their apparent assent to the contract was not genuine. There are several instances in which the law has recognized such a lack of assent.

Mistake

Mistakes can be unilateral (made by just one party) or mutual (made by both parties). Most mistakes do not release a person from a contract. All unilateral mistakes of fact, such as a failure to read a contract, result in the contract remaining valid. Unilateral mistakes of law, for instance a failure to realize that sales tax must be paid on the item purchased, also result in the contract remaining valid. The same is true of mutual, also called bilateral, mistakes of law. However, mutual mistakes of fact as to the identity of the subject matter result in the contract being considered void by the court, which will enforce *rescission* (a cancellation of the contract's obligations and the return to each party of what he or she has put into the contract). Note that a mutual mistake of fact as to the value of the subject matter (for example, you think a painting is a Picasso worth $5,000, and the other party thinks it is an Adamson worth $50) will still result in the contract you negotiated being considered valid by the courts.

Concealment

As a general rule, a person negotiating a contract is not under a duty to voluntarily reveal everything known about the subject matter. The resulting contract is valid regardless. If the other party or parties to the contract want to know something, they are free to ask. However, some contracts are formed between parties in relationships dependent on trust. In these *confidential relationships*, the law recognizes a duty to reveal all significant facts. Confidential relationships include attorney-client, physician-patient, and child-parent. "Silence when it is one's duty to speak," as the law puts it, can render a contract voidable by the party from whom the information is withheld.

Misrepresentation and Fraud

A **misrepresentation**, an innocent misstatement of a significant fact by a party, makes the resulting contract voidable by the party deceived. If the misrepresentation is made recklessly or intentionally in order to get the other party to enter into the contract and the other party does so without a good way to check on the untruth, the act would be considered **fraud**. In a case of fraud, an injured party may avoid the contract and seek damages.

Undue Influence and Duress

Mistake, concealment, misrepresentation, and fraud all deal with the quality of information provided or available to the contracting parties. Undue influence and duress deny contractual parties their ability to make reasonable choices about contracting, regardless of the quality and quantity of a party's factual knowledge.

With *undue influence*, the dominating party to a confidential relationship pressures the dominated party into a contract that benefits the former. An example would be an attorney selling a wealthy client the attorney's yacht at double the market price due to the carryover of the attorney's control of the client's legal matters. Such a contract is voidable by the dominated party.

With *duress*, a wrongful threat denies a person free will to contract. Such threats include those of bodily harm or death made against contracting parties or their immediate families, threats against a contracting party's home, or a threat to bring a criminal action against a contracting party. Note that a threat of a civil suit or of economic harm, such as "sign the contract or you'll never

Cross-Cultural Relationships

CONTRACT VERSUS COMMAND

The economic systems of many countries that previously relied on central government planning to drive production of goods and services have changed. Market economies, which allow individuals political freedom to choose their leaders and economic freedom to enter into contracts to satisfy their needs and wants, have been shown to be superior in the long run. They have replaced command economies in the former Soviet Union and much of Eastern Europe. In China, however, although controls on the economy have been greatly lessened, political control has remained in the hands of a few aging leaders.

Think Critically

Do you think the shift to market economies in Eastern Europe and the former Soviet Union was the result of an inability of central planners to control their economies or was it caused by a lack of understanding of basic human nature? Does China's prosperity indicate an even better pathway to follow? Give reasons for your answers.

do business in this town again," is not considered legal duress. Should one of the types of bona fide legal duress be proven, however, the contract is voidable by the party subjected to that duress.

Unconscionability

All of the problems with genuineness of assent discussed so far are individual ones. Courts also have had to deal with cases in which fully informed, capable individuals have, out of necessity, entered contracts that gave lopsided advantages to the other parties. To somehow grant relief from such unfair bargains, the courts had to formulate a new doctrine known as unconscionability. An *unconscionable contract* is one entered into as a result of the greatly unequal bargaining power of one party, who makes a take-it-or-leave-it offer to the other party who has no viable market alternative. If the resulting contract is grossly unfair to the weaker party, the offending section of the contract is void.

CheckPOINT

Name three confidential relationships that could be the basis for an undue influence claim?

_____

_____

Think Critically

1. The typical age of majority to contract is 18, yet 16-year-olds are licensed to drive, a life-and-death responsibility. How can this be justified?

   _____

   _____

2. What should society do with minors who knowingly use their protected status to injure others in bargains? For example, minors may buy luxury items, harm or sell them, and then avoid the contract to get their money back.

   _____

   _____

3. Why should we give any special protected status to those who voluntarily become intoxicated?

   _____

   _____

   _____

4. What problems would we incur if we let people out of contracts when there was a mutual mistake of fact as to the value of the subject matter?

   _____

   _____

   _____

   _____

5. What relationships, other than those named in the text, could or should be considered "confidential relationships" in the context of the laws regarding undue influence?

   _____

   _____

Make Academic Connections

6. **Research** As far as their contracts to perform and their compensation for doing so, child stars in Hollywood have their own special status under the law. What is that status, and why was it granted to them?

7. **Geography** On a map of the United States, color-code the states according to the ages of majority to contract, vote, and drink alcoholic beverages. Use the Internet or library to find the information.

JUMP START

A criminal in Arkansas paid a bribe to a judge for favorable treatment. When the judge still sentenced the criminal to the maximum allowed by law, the criminal sued to recover the bribe. The criminal noted that his action was not anywhere near the level of detriment to society that the judge's action was, and that it would be wrong for the judge to be enriched by his actions. Do you think the courts of Arkansas upheld the contract and allowed the criminal to recover his money? Why or why not?

GOALS

Identify contracts that are illegal

Recognize when a writing is required to prove a contract

KEY TERMS

usury, p. 52

statute of frauds, p. 55

Legality of Contracts

Agreements can be void and unenforceable if they involve contracting for an illegal act. For example, suppose Sam contracted with Murder Incorporated to shoot his ex-girlfriend but refused to pay after the homicide had been committed. Murder Incorporated could not win a suit against him for breach of contract. The contract is void and unenforceable because it is an illegal agreement.

Some contracts can involve a violation of the law and yet be enforceable. If you ordered stationery from a shop whose business license had expired, the shop would be in technical violation of the law for engaging in business without the proper license. If the shop breaches the contract, could you sue and recover? Yes you could, despite the illegality of the shop's operation.

It is both important and difficult to tell when a contract is unenforceable due to problems with legality. However, even though there is no absolute rule to resolve this issue, there are four basic indicators.

1. Statutes sometimes explicitly state that certain contracts are unenforceable. For example, most states have statutes that make private betting contracts unenforceable.

2. Courts look at the impact on public welfare of a violation of a statute related to the contract. Even though the homicide statute says nothing about the enforceability of contracts to murder, courts would rule them void because they have a big impact—the possible loss of a life—on the public welfare.

3. Courts look at how directly the contract and the violation of the statute are connected. In the Murder Incorporated example, they are directly related because the contract was for a homicide. In the business license example, the contract for stationery had little to do with the license. This would change if, for example, the license was to practice medicine and the contract was for brain surgery.

4. Courts look at how involved the parties are in the violation of a statute. In the murder contract, one party committed the murder and the other paid for the murder. This is deep involvement in violation of a homicide statute. On the other hand, when you ordered stationery, you were completely unaware that the shop's business license had expired. There is no direct involvement on your part in violation of the law.

The four factors above play a role in determining a court's response to the following situations involving different levels of illegality.

Illegal Gambling

Gambling, known at common law as an illegal lottery, involves an agreement with three elements. These include the consideration paid to participate, a chance to win based solely on luck rather than on skill, and a prize for one or more winners. Most states either forbid or regulate gambling. Typically, they have statutes that make gambling agreements void except those specifically sanctioned by the state.

Usurious Interest

Lending money at an interest rate higher than the maximum allowable rate set by state law, about 18 percent at the current time, is termed **usury**. State penalties for usury vary. In some states, the lender cannot collect some or all of the interest. However, the borrower must usually repay the principal. In other states, the entire loan agreement is considered void if the interest rate is excessive. Note that this rate is for borrowing money, not expanding the borrower's purchasing power by entering into a credit card agreement where the interest rates may be double the usury rates.

In addition, a recent Supreme Court decision now allows even higher rates, topping out at around an annualized 250 percent, to be charged on relatively small loans (up to $1,500 in most states and usually referred to as payday, cash-advance, or paycheck loans). Also, in most states, pawn shops are now permitted to charge similar rates on their secured loans. By comparison,

DID YOU KNOW ?

Even though gambling was allowed by statute in Nevada, for years the courts of that state could not be used to enforce gambling contracts. However, this has now changed.

however, realize that if your bank covers an overdraft of $100 and charges you a $25 insufficient funds charge on your next statement, the annualized rate is approximately 300 percent.

Illegal Discrimination

Some agreements are unenforceable because they violate anti-discrimination statutes. For example, an agreement between a motel chain and a local manager to not accept guests of a particular national origin would be unenforceable because it violates the federal Civil Rights Act of 1964. Agreements also may be illegal as violations of the Constitution. For example, a contract between a residential subdivision developer and a homebuyer that forbids the buyer to sell to a member of a particular race would be unenforceable. This contract violates the Fourteenth Amendment to the Constitution.

Obstruction of Legal Procedures

Agreements that delay or prevent justice are void. Examples include promises to do the following.

- Pay a nonexpert witness in a trial to testify, or pay for false testimony

- Bribe jurors

- Refrain from informing on or prosecuting an alleged crime in exchange for money or other valuable consideration (called *compounding a crime*)

A court or prosecutor may make the severity of a penalty dependent upon whether a criminal makes restitution, such as returning a stolen car.

Lack of Required Competency License

All states require that persons in certain occupations and businesses pass exams and receive a license to ensure that they are competent. Those who are engaged in trades, such as barbers, plumbers, and electrical wiring installers, typically require a *competency license*. Professionals such as physicians, teachers, lawyers, and pharmacists must have competency licenses as well. Real estate brokers, insurance agents, and building contractors are subject to such regulation. Persons who lack the required competency license may not enforce the contracts they make in doing the regulated work.

In contrast, some licenses are *revenue licenses*, such as a license to do business in a particular city. The purpose of a revenue license is to raise revenue rather than to protect the public. Contracts made by businesspeople who fail to obtain a revenue license are still considered valid. Typically, the only penalty for failure to get such a license is a higher fee when the license is later obtained.

Photodisc/Getty Images

What is the purpose of a competency license?

Negative Effects on Marriage

The law encourages marriage and family by making agreements that harm or interfere with marriage unenforceable. For example, Mimi is an illegal immigrant and Evan is a U.S. citizen. It would be an illegal contract if Mimi agreed to pay Evan $5,000 in exchange for his promise to marry her so she could obtain citizenship. A father's promise to pay his daughter for not marrying would be unenforceable as well.

Unreasonable Restraint of Trade

Our economic system is based on the concept of free and open competition. This creates profits for producers who benefit consumers the most. Both state and federal laws seek to prevent monopolies and combinations that restrict competition unreasonably.

Price Fixing When competing firms agree on the same price to be charged for a product or service, this injures consumers. It deprives them of the lower prices which competition would produce. *Price fixing* is a crime under federal law. Agreements to fix prices are therefore unenforceable.

One form of price fixing is *bid rigging*. This occurs when competitors who bid on jobs agree that one bidder will have the lowest bid for a particular job. It is illegal because typically the bid riggers take turns being the lowest bidder and set the price of the lowest bid higher than if there were real competition.

Resale Price Maintenance Manufacturers engage in *resale price maintenance* when they want retailers to sell their product at particular prices. Identifying a "suggested retail price" is legal. However, manufacturers may not agree or contract with retailers to sell the product at a particular price because that would involve two parties fixing the price. On the other hand, manufacturers can identify a suggested price and refuse to sell to retailers who do not adhere to the price.

Allocation of Markets The same injury to competition produced by price fixing can be achieved if competitors divide markets between themselves. This practice is known as *allocation of markets*. For example, if Ford automobile dealers in a state agree that they will not sell to residents outside the county where their dealership is located, this eliminates price competition for Ford automobiles and injures consumers. Therefore, agreements to allocate markets are illegal and unenforceable.

Covenants Not to Compete Price fixing and market allocations are agreements not to compete. One type of agreement not to compete is sometimes enforceable. When persons are hired, they may agree that they will not compete with their employer after the employment terminates. These covenants not to compete become illegal if they are unreasonable in

- Time period for the limitation
- Geographic area to which the limitation applies
- Employer's interest protected by the limitation

Rector and four other employees of Paramount Termite Control Company signed a noncompete contract. The employees agreed that for two years after leaving Paramount's employment, they would not solicit business from any customer of Paramount for the purpose of providing pest control services. Later, the five employees resigned from Paramount and immediately began working for a Paramount competitor that solicited business in counties prohibited by the noncompete agreement. Paramount brought suit against its former employees and the competitor to enforce the noncompete agreement.

THINK CRITICALLY
Do you think Paramount should succeed in this case? Why or why not?

An agreement not to compete for 20 years would likely be illegal. Often an agreement not to compete anywhere in the United States is ruled to be illegal. In contrast, an agreement not to engage in the printing business for two years in the city or county where the former employer is located probably would be enforceable. The employer's interests protected by the covenant not to compete must be significant. Trade secrets are the most commonly recognized employer interest.

CheckPOINT

Give two examples of agreements that unreasonably restrain trade.

_____

_____

_____

When a Written Contract Is Required

Although, in most cases, oral contracts are legally valid, binding, and enforceable, proving them in court is often impossible due to the complexity and number of terms or conflicting testimony as to the terms' substance. Therefore, it is always a good idea to put an important contract in writing. In addition, the law in most states identifies distinct situations in which, should one party to such a contract deny its existence, a written contract signed by that party is required to enforce the contract. Without such a writing, even the most reliable witnesses testifying to the contract's existence and to its terms will not give the court the power to enforce it. Typically, a law called the **statute of frauds** specifies the situations that require a writing as follows.

How might the statute of frauds apply to a marriage?

1. When a right or interest in real property, such as land and buildings, is being transferred. These rights and interests may include title, use, possession, and others.

2. When the contract cannot be performed within a year. This rule does not apply to situations where it is unlikely that the contract will be performed in a year. Instead it is applied when the contract absolutely cannot be performed in that time span.

3. When a sale of goods valued at more than $500 is involved. Note the providing of services is not considered under this rule.

4. When someone makes a promise to a creditor to stand good for the debts of another. If the promise is made to the debtor, however, a writing is not required.

5. When someone in charge of an estate makes a promise to stand good for the estate's debts.

6. When promises other than the exchange of the traditional vows are given in consideration of marriage.

CheckPOINT

What is the purpose of the statute of frauds?

_____

_____

_____

Think Critically

1. Why should the law refuse to enforce gambling or bribery contracts?

_____

_____

_____

_____

2. Why would a price-fixing agreement that sets prices substantially lower than the current market price be illegal?

_____

_____

_____

_____

3. Should the law refuse to enforce a contract you make with a retailer that you know does not have a valid business license? Why or why not?

_____

_____

_____

_____

4. Concerning the six situations in which most states require a writing under their statute of frauds, is there a common thread between them? If so, what is it?

_____

_____

_____

_____

Make Academic Connections

5. **Sociology** In what other areas do you think the courts should refuse to enforce contracts? Justify your answers.

6. **Research** Research the limits on interest rates on loans of money, large and small, secured and unsecured, and credit card purchases imposed by at least 10 states. Record your findings on a spreadsheet. Then write a one-page report about the economic significance of these limits.

Chapter Summary

2.1 Contract Law Basics
A. There are six essential elements for a legally valid and enforceable contract.
B. An understanding of various terms is necessary to master contract law.

2.2 Offer and Acceptance
A. An offer is a proposal of a bargain or exchange to another party or parties.
B. An offer can be terminated by revocation, expiration, rejection by the offeree, counteroffers, death, or insanity.
C. Consideration is what the offeror demands and generally must receive in order for the offer to be legally binding against him or her.

2.3 Capacity to Contract
A. A lack of capacity to contract on the part of one or more parties due to minority, insanity, or intoxication may result in a contract being unenforceable.
B. Genuineness of assent may not be present due to mistake, concealment, misrepresentation, fraud, undue influence, duress, and unconscionability.

2.4 Legality of Contracts
A. Whether or not courts will enforce illegal contracts is dependent on several considerations.
B. If the existence of the contract is denied by the party against whom enforcement is sought, the statute of frauds determines when a writing is required to overcome the party's denial.

Vocabulary Builder

Choose the term that best fits the definition. Write the letter of the answer in the space provided. Some terms may not be used.

_____ 1. A contract that has its terms set down in a clear-cut fashion, either orally or in writing

_____ 2. Proposal of a bargain or exchange to another party or parties

_____ 3. Lending money at a rate higher than the maximum allowable rate set by state law

_____ 4. An innocent misstatement of a significant fact

_____ 5. A contract that is legally binding and enforceable

_____ 6. What the offeror demands, and generally must receive, in order to make the offer legally enforceable against the offeror

_____ 7. Things needed to maintain life and lifestyle

_____ 8. The agreement by an offeree to the terms of an offer

a. acceptance
b. consideration
c. contract
d. express contract
e. fraud
f. implied contract
g. misrepresentation
h. necessaries
i. offer
j. ratification
k. statute of frauds
l. usury
m. valid contract

Review Concepts

Point Your
Browser
www.cengage.com/
school/business/21biz

9. What are the differences between valid, voidable, and void contracts?

_____

_____

_____

_____

10. Why does the law distinguish between executed and executory contracts?

_____

_____

_____

11. Explain how the terms offeror, promisor, and obligor apply to a contract.

_____

_____

_____

_____

12. What is the difference between a unilateral and a bilateral contract?

_____

_____

_____

13. What purpose does knowing the six essential elements of a contract serve?

_____

_____

_____

14. List four ways in which a valid offer may be terminated before acceptance.

_____

_____

_____

_____

15. What is the significance of contractual consideration?

_____

_____

_____

16. For what reasons may a person be denied contractual capacity?

_____

_____

_____

17. What circumstances can make an apparent assent to a contract voidable? void?

_____

_____

_____

18. List the various times when a writing is required to prove a contract in accordance with the statute of frauds.

_____

_____

_____

Apply What You Learned

19. Are food, clothing, and shelter the only necessaries in your life? What are some possible additions to the list?

_____

_____

20. Should social contracts be enforced? Should damages be awarded for their breach? Why or why not?

_____

_____

_____

21. How would you change the definition of contractual capacity if you had the power to do so?

_____

_____

_____

22. Can you formulate a uniform rule for the status of illegal contracts? If so, what is it? If not, why not?

_____

_____

_____

23. If you make a promise to your sister's creditor that you will pay her debt if she is unable to do so, does your promise need to be in writing? Why or why not?

_____

_____

_____

Make Academic Connections

24. **Environment** What sort of protective terms can you devise that could be placed in every contract that might affect the environment?

_____

_____

_____

25. **Marketing** Read the fine print in car sales and lease ads. Do you understand it? Is it a barrier to entering into a contract to buy a car? Why or why not?

_____

_____

_____

26. **Entertainment Law** A child movie star of 16 is given $30,000 from his earnings to buy his own car. Does he have the capacity to contract for it?

_____

_____

_____

27. **Communication** Write a one-page report evaluating the nature of offers and acceptances made over the Internet. Often many terms are not discussed before the deal is closed. Is this a good or a bad idea? Why?

Ethical Dilemma

28. You are the parent of a 10-year-old child who has a truly amazing singing voice, but she is very shy. A major movie studio offers her a contract that, in part, requires her to be filmed singing the national anthem before some 60,000 baseball fans. You know that she could be greatly harmed psychologically in attempting to do so and by the publicity that follows, but the studio contract calls for her to be paid $150,000 for her efforts, which would likely pay for her college education. Should you enter into the contract on her behalf? Explain your answer.

_____

_____

_____

_____

_____

The Law of Property

Careers in Business Law

BLIZZARD ENTERTAINMENT

Blizzard Entertainment is a developer of video games headquartered in Irvine, California. Blizzard's most notable creation is a massively multiplayer online role-playing game (MMORPG) entitled World of Warcraft. The company was founded in 1991 by three gamers barely a year after they graduated from UCLA. It currently employs around 2,700 with revenues exceeding $1 billion per year.

Copyright Attorneys at Blizzard must understand the legal aspects of obtaining and protecting intellectual property rights in the company's constantly evolving products. They need a law degree and hands-on experience in the field of gaming, especially in writing games. An undergraduate degree in computers with an emphasis on higher-level computer languages is desirable.

Think Critically

1. Why do Copyright Attorneys at Blizzard need both a legal and a gaming background?
2. Do you think securing copyrights for gaming products would be more difficult than protecting them?

Project Objectives

- Develop a sense of what property is
- Appreciate the importance of property in your life

Getting Started

Read the Project Process below. Decide how you will get the needed materials or information.

Photodisc/Getty Images

Project Process

3.1 Consider various types of property that you or your family owns. How was this property acquired? Which family member actually owns it? Why does this family member have such a right? What would happen to the property upon the death or divorce of your parents? What role could property or life insurance play in protecting your family?

3.2 List the real property you and your family own. What changes would occur in your life if this property were no longer yours?

3.3 List the bailments that you and your family use. Which are dependent on financial resources and which are not? What are the sources for the gratuitous bailments you enjoy? Could you replace the bailments if they were not available?

3.4 Consider the various types of intellectual property. Do you or your family have any property that is unprotected, such as songs, prose, poetry, inventions, or trademarks? How would you go about protecting this property?

Chapter Review

Project Wrap-up Create a chart of your real, personal, intellectual, and bailed property. Write a one-page report explaining which piece or type of property you own is most valuable to you and why.

Comstock Images/Jupiter Images

GOALS

Discuss the concept of property and its various types

Identify and explain how property is acquired and held

KEY TERMS

property, p. 64

real property, p. 65

personal property, p. 65

insurance, p. 70

 JUMP START

Eric purchased a new mini-laptop for use in his classes. It was very light (under a pound), did not use a mechanical hard drive, had wireless communication built in, and the keyboard folded out from the laptop's 4-by-8-inch frame. Eric's friend, Jeannie, who was working after school as a reporter for an online paper, noticed him using it in class. She asked if she could rent it to take notes at an upcoming city council meeting. Eric agreed. Later in the semester, Eric let a classmate use the laptop overnight to study from his notes for a test in one of the classes they had together. Can each of the three students claim a property interest in the laptop?

©Jenkedco, 2009/ Used under license from Shutterstock.com

The Concept of Property

What is property? Many of us think of property as things we can own, rent, or otherwise obtain some right or interest in. In the law, however, **property** refers to the rights and interests in things that society allows people to claim. The things can be tangible or intangible. Tangible things are those you can see and touch. You cannot see or touch intangible things. Note that property is not the items themselves, but the rights and interests in them. As reflected by the situation in *Jump Start,* many people can have an interest in the same property under our legal system. Each society decides what types of property rights its citizens can have.

Property Rights and Interests

The most important of the rights and interests that U.S. society recognizes is title. In property law, *title* means a legally endorsed claim to ultimate ownership. *Ownership*, in turn, refers to a bundle of rights, including title, allowing a person the full enjoyment of something. *Possession* is another property right. It allows the immediate control or power over something to the exclusion of all others. A third right, *use*, allows a person to employ something to achieve some result. Finally, the right of *alienation* allows a person to determine how to do away with something, such as by destroying, selling, or consuming it.

Types of Property

Property can be divided into several categories and subcategories. The most important are real property and personal property.

- **Real property** is rights and interests in land, buildings, and fixtures. *Fixtures* are tangible, movable things that become permanently attached to land and buildings.

- **Personal property** is rights and interests in basically anything that is not real property, tangible or intangible. A subcategory of personal property is *intellectual property*. It includes intangible property such as patents, copyrights, and trademarks. Another subcategory that involves tangible personal property is *bailment*. Both intellectual property and bailments are discussed later in the chapter.

TEAMWORK

Divide into small teams. Have each person consider the most valuable piece of property that he or she owns. Make a list of how each exercises his or her rights and interests of

- title
- possession
- use
- alienation

Brainstorm ways these rights and interests might be transferred or terminated.

CheckPOINT

Name the four rights an owner has to property.

_____

_____

Acquiring and Owning Property

You can acquire property through a wide variety of means. For example, you may acquire both real and personal property by contract, gift, or inheritance. In most instances, the acquisition of property rights by one party is the result of the termination of the corresponding rights of the previous owner. Intellectual property is the major exception and will be discussed later in the chapter.

Once property has been acquired, property owners need to be aware of the different forms of property ownership. Each form of ownership carries different risks and interests. Property owners must recognize the need to properly insure against these risks.

Acquiring Property by Contract

Any kind of property may be acquired, transferred, bought, or sold through the use of contracts.

Acquiring Property by Gift

A gift is a voluntary transfer of property from one party to another without consideration. Gifts are comprised of three elements: intent to give, delivery, and acceptance.

The person doing the giving is the *donor*. The recipient of the gift is the *donee*. The delivery may be actual or constructive. Actual delivery would involve the physical delivery of the subject matter of the gift, such as enclosing $50 in a birthday card and handing it to the donee. Constructive delivery involves an action that is representative of a physical delivery, such as putting the keys to a new car in a birthday card for the donee.

Acquiring Property by Inheritance

Real and personal property may be inherited from others after they die. If a valid will exists, it will specify who is to receive the properties of the person who died (referred to as the *decedent*). If a will does not exist, the courts will follow the instructions of the appropriate state statute to determine how the property is to be divided among the decedent's survivors. The inheritor, by will or by statute, is referred to in common usage as an *heir*.

If a person dies leaving a bona fide will, she or he is said to have died *testate*. The person making the will is therefore referred to as the *testator* if male or *testatrix* if female. If no will was left, the decedent is said to have died *intestate*. Regardless of whether the decedent died testate or intestate, the transfer of the decedent's property, called the *estate*, is placed under the control of a probate court. After the probate court ensures that the creditors of the decedent and other claimants against the estate have been satisfied, the remainder of the decedent's property will be distributed among his or her survivors.

In most instances, in order to be valid, a will must be shown to

- have been made by a person with proper mental capacity
- reflect the clear intent of the decedent
- be in writing signed by him or her in front of witnesses who will not inherit under the will

Some states recognize unwitnessed wills written and signed by the decedent's own hand. Oral wills are also deemed valid by some states but only for the distribution of the decedent's personal property.

Wills can be amended or revoked at any time by the testator or testatrix. In many states, life-changing events such as marriage, divorce, or the birth of a child lead to an automatic termination of a previously made will.

If a person dies without a will, state statutes determine who shall receive what portion of the property of the decedent. Generally, these intestacy statutes call for a surviving spouse to get one-third to one-half of the estate with the remainder being divided among the children. If there is no spouse or surviving children, the statutes allow for more distant relatives to receive an appropriate part of the estate. If the decedent leaves no inheritors, the estate will revert, or *escheat*, to the state.

Other Means of Acquiring Real Property

Property also may be acquired through adverse possession, eminent domain, or dedication.

- *Adverse possession* applies to acquiring the land of another by continuously occupying it for an extended period of time, usually 10 years. State laws differ slightly, but the occupation typically must be without the consent of the owner, visible to the public, and with some legal basis.

- Under *eminent domain* laws, each state has the power to take private real property for its use or a public use by a city, a person, an association, or a corporation.

- Land belonging to a private entity may be offered to a city, state, or other governmental body for its use or ownership. Such an offer of *dedication* must be accepted, however, or the transfer is not effective. Usually, a developer of a subdivision will offer to dedicate the roads and park areas of the development to the controlling governmental body in exchange for that body becoming responsible for maintaining them.

Why should the government be able to acquire property through eminent domain?

©Leo, 2009/ Used under license from Shutterstock.com

Other Means of Acquiring Personal Property

Personal property also may be acquired through accession, creation of intellectual property, or finding lost property.

- *Accession* is the right of an owner to an increase in the value of the property. For example, farm crops and the offspring of animals belong to the owner of the land and the animals.

- Authors, inventors, and others create their own intellectual property. Upon proper qualification, this type of property is protected by the common law and by the state and federal governments.

- Finders of *lost* or *mislaid property* may keep property that is truly lost; that is, the true owner has no idea where the property is. Mislaid property, or property placed somewhere but then forgotten, must remain with the party who controls the area where it was found. This is because the person who lost the property might remember where he or she mislaid it and return to get it. Anyone who loses property has the right to recover it from any finder. Also, when the finder knows who the true owner is, she or he has a duty to return it to that person. If the true owner is unknown, either the finder or the person controlling the area where the property was found may keep the item (and must exercise reasonable care of it) until the true owner appears. Most states allow the finder to obtain ownership by advertising the find over a period of time in "publications of general circulation," presuming the owner does not present himself as a result.

Forms of Property Ownership

The ownership of real property can be held in a variety of ways. *Ownership in severalty* exists when one person holds all rights and interests. There are also several forms of joint ownership that allow two or more people rights and interests in the same property.

All forms of co-ownership have two attributes in common. First, all co-owners have equal rights of possession of the property. Second, the co-owners have the right to partition. This *right of partition* allows any co-owner to require the division of the property among the co-owners. If the property is not divisible, such as an airplane or sailboat, it must be sold. The proceeds of the sale must then be divided among the co-owners.

The two most common forms of co-ownership are tenancy in common and joint tenancy. A *tenancy in common* allows unequal ownership shares, no right of survivorship (described below), and places no restrictions on the transfer of ownership. Therefore, any deceased owner's interest passes according to her or his will, if there is one. A *joint tenancy* features the *right of survivorship*. This right means that, under a time-tested legal rule, each of the co-owners are presumed to own all of the subject property at the same time. Thus if one dies, a remaining owner does not have to place the property in probate, which often results in delays and costs, because she or he has owned it all along. This is true even if the will of the deceased says otherwise. If a joint tenant transfers his or her interest in the property, the joint tenancy is dissolved and becomes a tenancy in common.

Tenancy by the Entireties In some states, another form of co-ownership exists, called a *tenancy by the entireties*. This tenancy exists only between husbands and wives and also features the right of survivorship. It provides a considerable advantage to the tenants (the husband and wife) because the creditor of one tenant cannot force the sale of the property to pay off the debt as the property is also owned by another. Therefore, lenders will almost always require both marital partners to sign as obligors on a loan. However, a divorce converts this tenancy into a tenancy in common. Finally, in some states, all property acquired by the wife or husband during the marriage is presumed to be *community property*. Each spouse owns a one-half interest in such property unless it has been received as a gift or an inheritance.

Effects of Divorce In addition to its effect on tenancy by the entireties, *divorce*—the legal termination of a marriage relationship—results in many changes on the property holdings of the couple involved. Divorce is distinct from the legal process of *annulment*, which is a legal means for declaring certain marriages null and void. These temporary and voidable unions can be terminated because of problems that existed from the beginning. These problems may include a refusal to have children and fraudulent grounds for the marriage contract, such as false statements regarding wealth, condition of pregnancy, disease, or age.

Unlike annulment, however, divorce terminates a valid marriage relationship and has become far more available since 1969 when Governor Ronald Reagan of California signed into law the first no-fault divorce statute. This statute eliminated the need for assessing and proving a grievance (such as adultery, desertion, or cruelty) against a spouse in order to secure a divorce. Instead, the divorce court acknowledges the right of a spouse to terminate a marriage unilaterally or mutually with the other spouse. Irreconcilable differences are typically cited as the reason under most state laws for the dissolution of the marriage.

Divorce in some states is preceded by a legal *separation* in which the spouses retain their marital rights and duties (unless altered by a negotiated separation agreement) but live apart. Often a separation agreement provides the basic material for the *divorce decree* (the court order or judgment officially dissolving the marriage). In it are terms covering the most important issues involved in a divorce: child custody, *child support* (the monetary payment by a parent to maintain a dependent child), *alimony* (the monetary payment by the wage earner of the family to maintain the other spouse), and division of marital property. Typically, even no-fault divorces take several months because time is needed to work out disagreements between the parties. In addition, many states, due to the high rates of divorce, require mandatory counseling of the parties before finalizing the matter with a divorce decree. Finally, a divorce decree is subject to alteration by the court if there is a significant change in circumstance of one or both of the parties.

Cross-Cultural Relationships

FOREIGN LAND OWNERSHIP IN COMMUNIST CUBA

Eager to attract foreign capital investments, the Marxist government of Cuba has recently allowed British and Canadian companies to develop several resort properties around the island. Building literally thousands of hotel rooms, hundreds of bungalows, and recreational beach and golf facilities, the companies are investing hundreds of millions of dollars, which they intend to recoup during 75-year leaseholds. A significant amount of the investment capital comes from sources in the Middle East, including nearly $50 million from Dubai. Further permissive rules are rumored to be under consideration to allow sales to developers (with actual ownership) of the now crumbling colonial era buildings. These changes are supposedly being authored by the current leader, Raul Castro. Raul is the brother of the revolutionary Fidel Castro, who almost immediately confiscated private property after seizing power in 1959. Such property is considered a factor of production under communism and, therefore, is to be owned by the people in the form of the state.

Think Critically

What factors do you think have influenced the change in Cuban policies as to the ownership of private property, especially real estate? What factors might keep the Cuban government from making further changes?

Why is it important to insure against certain types of risk?

Insuring Property

Whatever property we might have, there is always the danger of unexpected loss. In such a situation, insurance is vital. **Insurance** is a contractual obligation taken on by one party to *indemnify* (make good) the loss incurred by another party. Insurance is available to cover risks of all types, except the risk of a loss from doing business. Seagoing vessels can be insured; movie producers can obtain "completion" insurance; baseball pitchers can insure their pitching hand; automobile drivers/owners can insure against collision, liability, vandalism, and many other risks; homeowners can insure against fire; business partners can insure against the death of a partner; and so on. The list is practically endless. The party indemnifying another is the *insurer*. The party indemnified is the *insured*. The party to receive payment under the *policy* (insurance contract) is the *beneficiary*. The amount paid for the insurance coverage is called the *premium*. The main types of insurance are life and casualty.

Life Insurance With *life insurance*, the beneficiary is paid a set amount upon the death of the party whose life is insured. To take out a life insurance policy on another person, the policyholder must have an *insurable interest* (the potential to sustain loss if the insured dies). Each of us has such an interest in ourselves, and spouses may insure one another. However, brothers and sisters are not generally considered to have an insurable interest in one another. The insurable interest need only be present at the time the policy is taken out, not at the time of loss. This is unlike property insurance, where the insurable interest must be shown at the time the policy is written and at the time of a loss. This prevents speculation, or betting on the occurrence of losses.

Casualty Insurance The second major type of insurance, *casualty insurance*, provides protection in situations where the accidental, intentional, or negligent acts of others or acts of nature result in a loss. For example, if your car is hit by a meteorite, casualty insurance would cover the damages.

CheckPOINT

Name three ways, other than by contract, gift, or inheritance, of acquiring real property and personal property.

_____

_____

Think Critically

1. Would a private individual be able to own real property in a communist country? If not, why? If so, what restrictions might be placed on this ownership?

_____

_____

_____

2. What is the most important right or interest in property? Explain.

_____

_____

_____

3. Why should the law allow adverse possession? What governmental purpose does it serve?

_____

_____

_____

4. What is the difference between an annulment and a divorce?

_____

_____

_____

Make Academic Connections

5. **Communication** Through the Internet, contact three students in various countries around the world. Ask them if there is any type of property that citizens of their country cannot own, such as land, factories, firearms, and so on. Then ask them to give the rationale for such rules. Write a paragraph comparing your findings and offering explanations for the results.

6. **Research** Determine the role insurance plays in your life. Ask your parents what types of insurance they carry and why. Consult an insurance agent to determine whether or not the agent feels the breadth and amount of coverage is adequate. If it is not considered adequate, record what additional coverages are recommended and why.

7. **Geography** Examine ten of your family's possessions to determine the country in which each item was made. Use a world map and mark the country and type of property. What conclusions can you draw from your display?

JUMP START

Jennifer purchased a flat screen, high-definition television for the living room of her apartment. Shortly thereafter, her father built a new mantle for the fireplace in the apartment and encased the television in the wood paneling above it. When Jennifer received a job transfer and needed to move, the landlord, Mike, maintained that she could not take the television with her because it now belonged to him as the owner of the building. Is he correct?

©Monkey Business Images, 2009/ Used under license from Shutterstock.com

What Is Real Property?

Real property, or *realty*, is comprised of land, buildings, and fixtures. Real property extends from the farthest reaches of the atmosphere, across the surface of the subject area, and down to the center of the earth. The rights to drill or mine under the surface are referred to as *mineral rights*. In some states, mineral rights can be transferred independently of surface rights.

Fixtures

Fixtures are a special category of real property. *Fixtures* are items that are at first considered personal property. They become realty when they are permanently attached to real property. When the items are permanently attached, the ownership passes to the owner of the real property. Exceptions to this are situations involving *trade fixtures*. An example of a trade fixture would be a built-in pizza oven in an Italian restaurant at a shopping mall. These fixtures are never intended to become the property of the owner of the real property. When the lease ends, the tenant can remove such property.

Powers and Limitations of Real Property Ownership

The powers of ownership of real property vary with the type of estate, or bundle of rights, received upon taking ownership. The words used in the deed, or document by which rights and interests in real property are transferred, control this. The party who transfers the ownership powers is the *grantor*. The party receiving the powers is the *grantee*. When an estate is transferred from a grantor to a grantee by deed, the transaction is known as a *conveyance*.

There are two types of deeds. A *quitclaim deed* transfers only the rights and interests that the grantor has in the real property. If the grantor does not have any such rights and interests, the deed is worthless. With a *warranty deed*, at a minimum, the grantor promises that she or he has good, clear title. In most cases, the grantor also promises that the property is free from adverse claims and that the grantor has the right to convey it.

Types of Estates in Land and the Powers They Convey

Estates in land vary from absolute ownership to various conditional ownerships or use.

Fee Simple Absolute An estate that incorporates all ownership rights is called a *fee simple absolute*. The owner of it exercises all the powers allowed by law in the real property.

Conditional Estate An estate that allows ownership as long as a condition is satisfied or goes unviolated is called a *conditional estate*. For example, land willed to a daughter "as long as it is used for an animal shelter" would be such an estate. Should the land no longer be utilized in the manner required, ownership would revert (return) to the estate of the decedent.

Life Estate An estate that typically allows its owner the rights of possession, use, and profit for the duration of a particular person's life, usually the holder, is called a *life estate*. The holder of a life estate cannot waste (destroy or spoil) the value of the property or permanently dispose of it.

Nonfreehold Estate An estate that involves an agreement to allow exclusive possession and use of the realty is called a *nonfreehold estate*. Such estates are more commonly referred to as *tenancies* or *leaseholds*. There are four basic types of nonfreehold estates.

1. A *periodic tenancy* is for a renewable period of time with the rent due at stated intervals. These leaseholds in real property can be month to month or week to week. Renewal of the lease is automatic unless a termination notice is given by the *landlord/lessor* (the party creating the estate) or the *tenant/ lessee* (the party using the estate).

2. A *tenancy for years* is a leasehold for a definite period of time. It is referred to by this name even though the period of the lease can be for more or less than a year. At the end of the lease period, this tenancy terminates automatically without any further notice being required.

Which type of tenancy is common among apartment tenants?

3. A *tenancy at sufferance* is created when a tenant does not leave on the day the lease ends. The tenant is thereafter referred to as a *holdover tenant* and can be held liable for rent for the holdover period or can be *evicted*, or dislodged from the premises by the landlord.

4. A *tenancy at will* is created when a party possesses land with the owner's permission but without agreement as to rent or duration of the tenancy. Such a leasehold may be terminated at any time with minimal notice from either party.

Whatever estate is involved, the tenant must be allowed exclusive use and possession of the premises. Unless restricted by the terms of the lease, the tenant may transfer all of her or his rights under the lease to a third party. This is referred to as an *assignment of the lease*. A tenant transferring only part of his rights under a lease to a third person is referred to as *subletting*.

Both subletting and assignment may be prohibited or made subject to the landlord's permission in the lease. Regardless of whether the lease has been sublet or assigned, the original tenant is liable for the fulfillment of his or her duties under the lease unless released by the landlord. These duties include paying rent, taking reasonable care of the property, and exercising a duty of due care (reasonable and appropriate care) toward those who enter onto the property.

The landlord has duties as well. These may be prescribed by the government, in the lease, or by the common law. Governmental duties are usually set down in a *housing code* that details the standards for the condition of the premises provided by the landlord. These standards may include no exposed wiring, private bathrooms in every unit, and no leaks in the roof. Under the common law, if the landlord does not provide livable premises and the tenant is forced to leave, a *constructive eviction* has occurred. As a result, the landlord may be liable to pay for the tenant's alternative housing.

CheckPOINT

Are fixtures always considered real property? Why or why not?

_____

_____

©ostill, 2009/ Used under license from Shutterstock.com

Restrictions on Real Property

There are many restrictions on the use of the powers inherent in real property ownership. *Restrictive covenants* included in previous deeds sometimes "run with the land." This means they bind later owners to their terms. Zoning ordinances by cities or counties also may restrict the real property owners' rights. *Variances*, or exceptions to zoning requirements, may be granted by a governmental body if a property owner shows, for example, hardship or lack of injury to others.

Real property also may be subject to *easements*. Utility companies usually employ these irrevocable rights to gain access across one party's land to reach others with its services. Easements also may be given to a neighbor who cannot reach his or her property without going across another's land.

Certain real property owners may give temporary, revocable rights to occupy or use their property to people or businesses. These are referred to as *licenses*. Such licenses are personal, nontransferable, not inheritable, and not considered an estate in land. A ticket to watch a movie in a theater is an example. If a patron is too loud or becomes unruly, the patron's license can be revoked. Thereafter, the patron can be classified as a trespasser and removed. A *trespasser* is someone who is on another's property without any right, authority, express or implied invitation, permission, or license.

Of course, even trespassers have rights. A real property owner is charged with the duty of refraining from doing them intentional harm. A property owner owes a similar duty to a licensee and must warn licensees of known dangers, such as guard dogs. Finally, to a *business invitee*—a person who comes onto property to do business with the owner—the property owner has several duties: to refrain from doing intentional harm, to warn of known dangers, and to conduct inspections to discover such dangers. Therefore, a supermarket has a duty to conduct inspections of its premises to find dangerous situations, such as wet floors, and warn customers of them.

Why is an amusement park ticket considered a license?

CheckPOINT

Name three types of restrictions that may be placed on real property.

_____

_____

Think Critically

1. Real property law is considered to be the most settled, unalterable, and out of date of any area of the law. What reasons can you give for this?

_____

_____

_____

2. Why should trade fixtures be legally removable at the end of a tenancy?

_____

_____

_____

_____

3. What conditions might result in a constructive eviction?

_____

_____

_____

4. Your landlord wants to show your apartment to a prospective renter on a day you need undisturbed use of it. There is no term in the lease regarding such tours. Could the landlord legally compel you to let it be shown that day? Why or why not?

_____

_____

_____

5. Why should the original tenant remain responsible on a lease that has been assigned?

_____

_____

_____

Make Academic Connections

6. **Ecology** Research and examine the history of the discharge and/or storage of toxic waste in this country. Prepare a presentation that examines how real property rights come in conflict with protecting the country's natural resources.

7. **Marketing** Read five advertisements in a newspaper. What potential problems, in the way of duties to business invitees, do you see for the various businesses? Write a one-page report about your conclusions.

JUMP START

John and Sharon are team drivers. They rented a truck from Rent-a-Rig to haul a load of apples from an orchard in Missouri to various markets in New York. Their contract with Rent-a-Rig called for them to drop off the truck to another Rent-a-Rig outlet in Buffalo from where they would fly back to Missouri. Was the rental a bailment? Why or why not?

GOALS

Identify the various bailments

Describe the duties associated with each bailment

KEY TERMS

bailment, p. 77

fungible, p. 79

Digital Vision/Getty Images

What Is a Bailment?

One area of vital importance in property law is the possession of personal property with or without the right to use it. This is the field of bailments. A **bailment** is the temporary transfer of possession and control of personal property subject to an agreement that typically calls for the subject property to be returned to the person creating the bailment at a later time or passed on to a specified third party. Bailments have four characteristics.

1. The subject is personal property.

2. There is a temporary transfer of *possession*.

3. There is a temporary transfer of *control*.

4. The parties intend the goods to be returned to the person giving up possession or passed on to a specified third party as per the agreement.

If you lend your pen to a friend for a moment, you are involved in the legal relation of bailment. The transaction is neither a sale nor a gift, because your friend is obligated to return the pen to you. You are the *bailor*, or the party who gives up possession and control of the property. Your friend is the *bailee*, or the party who receives possession and control. Usually property is bailed by the person with title to the goods. However, it may be bailed by any person in possession. This includes the owner's agent or employee. It also includes a custodian, a finder, or even a thief.

Types of Bailments

There are two basic types of bailments, actual and constructive. In an *actual bailment*, bailees receive and accept the goods themselves. Thus, when you rent a truck from Rent-A-Rig and drive off, you receive and accept the truck in bailment. (Note that a *constructive delivery* occurs when the bailee receives and accepts a *symbol* of the personal property, such as the keys to a truck that is located elsewhere, instead of the property itself. However, the resulting bailment is still considered an actual bailment.)

A *constructive bailment* occurs when the law (usually by court order) imposes upon someone holding another's personal property a bailee's duty to take due care of it until it can be delivered to another party. A bank holding money in dispute during a divorce is an example of a constructive bailment.

Requirements of a Bailment

Does a bailment exist when you hand over your car keys to a parking valet? Explain.

In order for a bailment to arise, both *possession* and *control* of the goods must shift from the bailor to the bailee. Disputes often arise over cars left in parking lots. Suppose a car owner drives into a lot, parks the car, and keeps the key. She can later drive the car away without permission of an attendant. While the driver may have given up possession, she did not give up control. She has the keys and can drive away without the attendant's permission. In this case there is no bailment. There *is* a bailment, however, if an attendant takes possession of the car and gives the owner a claim check. The owner must present the claim check to get the car back. In this situation, both possession and control have been given to the bailee.

It is also possible for a person to have temporary control of another's personal property, yet not have a bailment. This occurs with *custody*. For example, a person hired to guard the paintings in an art museum has custody, but is not a bailee. A clerk using an employer's computer in the company offices is not a bailee. The owners of the art and the computer never gave complete control of the goods to the employees. They authorized the employees to guard or use the goods, but they retained control over them.

The bailor and bailee must intend that the goods be returned to the bailor or to a designated third party. Many bailments involve such third parties. For instance, a parent (bailor) ships a birthday gift to a child in college (third party) by using a public carrier (bailee).

Usually, the bailee must return or deliver the identical goods. The goods may be modified somewhat, as by agreed upon use, repairs, processing, or aging. Also, some goods are fungible. **Fungible** means that there is no difference between one unit of the goods and another. For example a unit of 500 gallons of 90-octane gasoline is the same as, or fungible with, another unit of 500 gallons of 90-octane gasoline. When the subject of the bailment is fungible, the bailee need only return the same *quantity* as received, not the exact same units of the goods.

TEAMWORK

Divide into two-person teams. Compete with the other teams to create the longest list of fungible goods.

CheckPOINT

What are the four characteristics of a bailment?

_____

_____

_____

Duties Associated with Bailments

Most legal problems with bailments arise when something happens to the goods while they are in the possession of the bailee. During this time, the type of bailment determines the degree of care the bailee must exercise over the goods. In general, the three levels of care are extraordinary, ordinary, and minimal. In a trial, the burden of showing that the level of care has been met rests with the bailee.

Extraordinary Care

Goods bailed with hotels and with common carriers, such as truck lines, UPS, and air freight haulers, are considered *extraordinary bailments*. In such a circumstance, the duty of care is extraordinary. Extraordinary care generally means the bailee will be strictly liable for any damage, loss, or injury to the goods. The only times this type of bailee is not liable is when the loss is caused by an act of war, unforeseeable "acts of God," or acts of police. Extraordinary care also is required of the bailee in a *gratuitous bailment*, where only the bailee benefits from the bailment. It would be a gratuitous bailment for the sole benefit of the bailee if you loaned your cell phone to a classmate without charge. Your

NET Bookmark

Shinn's Cleaners is one of the leading dry cleaning businesses in Little Rock, Arkansas. Access www.cengage.com/school/business/21biz and click on the link for Chapter 3. Read about Shinn's Cleaners and the services it offers, and then answer these questions: If you turn over some garments to Shinn's for dry cleaning, what kind of legal relationship have you created with the business? Are you the bailor or the bailee? Why? What level of care must Shinn's exercise over your garments? Explain.

www.cengage.com/school/business/21biz

classmate would therefore be strictly liable for any damage, loss, or injury to the cell phone until it was returned to you.

Ordinary Care

When consideration is given and received by both bailor and bailee, the arrangement is considered a *mutual benefit bailment* because both parties benefit. Thus, if you took your bicycle to a bicycle shop and paid $60 to have it repaired, you would receive the benefit of the repair, and the bicycle shop would receive the benefit of the $60. Mutual benefit bailments result from contracts, whereas gratuitous bailments do not because there is no exchange of consideration. A bailment of mutual benefit invokes only the duty of ordinary care. In most instances, *ordinary care* means that the bailee will only be liable if she has been *negligent*, or careless, in some fashion.

Minimal Care

Your neighbor is going on vacation and asks you to care for her dog while she is away. You agree to do it without charge. The neighbor drops "White Fang" off at your house just before she leaves for her around-the-world trip. This would be a gratuitous bailment for the sole benefit of the bailor. The duty of due care required of you would be minimal. In general, *minimal care* means that the bailee must not ignore, waste, or destroy the property.

Another type of bailment requiring only minimal care is *involuntary bailment*. Such a bailment arises without the consent of the bailee. This can happen when your neighbor's trash cans blow into your yard or a sail boat washes ashore on your beachfront property. This type of bailment can also arise when mail is delivered to the wrong addressee. In such cases, the involuntary bailment created requires only a minimal duty of care. However, for valuable property, the bailee must also make a minimal effort to identify the owner.

What level of care should you expect when you take something to a repair shop?

Digital Vision/Getty Images

Duty to Return the Goods

The *bailee's duty to return the property* compels the bailee to return the bailed property according to the terms of the bailment agreement. If the bailee is entitled to payment for the bailment but hasn't been paid, he or she may exercise a *bailee's lien* and retain possession until paid. If payment is delayed unreasonably, the bailee may sell the property to recover the fee and related costs.

Ending Bailments

The bailment ends when the time agreed upon by the parties has elapsed, when the agreed purpose has been accomplished, or when the parties mutually agree to end it. If no time of termination is stated, either party may end the bailment. Thus, the bailor might ask for the return of the property. Or, the bailee may no longer need the property and return it. Also, if the bailed property is destroyed or damaged so badly that it is not fit for the intended purpose, the bailment ends.

Death, insanity, or bankruptcy of one of the parties also may terminate the bailment under certain circumstances. Normally, however, if there is a contractual bailment for a fixed period, death or incapacity of a party does not end the relationship. The rights and duties of the deceased party are transferred by law to the estate of the deceased.

Photodisc/Getty Images

If you enter into a bailment by lending someone your car, how might the bailment be terminated?

COMMUNICATE

Consider a recent bailment situation in which you participated with a friend or acquaintance, such as with a borrowed/loaned video game, cell phone, or MP3 player. Write a paragraph summarizing your agreement with the person. Include the level of care required for the bailment. Also describe the duty to return the good and how the bailment was to be ended.

CheckPOINT

What standard of care is required in an involuntary bailment?

_____

_____

_____

Think Critically

1. You are starting up a company in the construction industry. How could bailments be of assistance to you?

   _____

   _____

2. Why should common carriers be required to take extraordinary care of the goods that are bailed to them?

   _____

   _____

3. What reasons can you give for the *bailee's lien*? Shouldn't the ability to sue in court for unpaid fees be enough?

   _____

   _____

   _____

4. You take your projection TV to be repaired. When the shop's technician notifies you to pick it up, he tells you that because it is over 10 years old, he was unable to get repair parts. Consequently, he substituted parts from more modern projection TVs and, unfortunately, blew the microchips in your set. The technician still wants $150 for labor. You refuse to pay and demand your TV set and damages. What standard of due care is involved? What do you think the shop's response will be? Can the repair shop sell your TV set to satisfy its charges? Why or why not?

   _____

   _____

   _____

   _____

Make Academic Connections

5. **Research** Go to various rental businesses and ask for copies of their contracts. For most firms, you should find that the contracts are lengthy and cannot be changed by bargaining with the local representatives. Compare the contracts. Write a one-page report on your conclusions.

6. **Business Math** Using spreadsheet software, make a list of furniture and other items of personal property that you would need to furnish a one-bedroom apartment. Call a business that offers such items for rent and inquire about its rates. Total the payments for the items you have listed. Then call a furniture store and find out how much it would cost to buy these items. Compare the total amounts and draw conclusions.

JUMP START

One evening, Francia and Britannia Chan decided to make a music video. They designed their own sets, choreographed costumes and movements, and composed the music. During the making of the video, they also developed a mechanism to let them control the camera angle selection as they performed. Finally, they drew a logo for Sibling Works, their own production and marketing organization. They planned to put the video on their organization's website as soon as they had finished editing it. What intellectual property protection would you recommend for their efforts?

©Iurii Davydov, 2009/ Used under license from Shutterstock.com

GOALS

Recognize the role of intellectual property in our society

Identify what kinds of intellectual property can be protected and how

KEY TERMS

intellectual property, p. 83

copyright, p. 83

trademark, p. 84

patent, p 85

trade secret, p. 86

Types of Intellectual Property

Personal property includes not only tangible, but also intangible property. Intellectual property is typically intangible; that is, one cannot see or touch it. **Intellectual property** includes copyrights, patents, trade secrets, service marks, and trademarks. Federal statutes generally govern the creation, use, and transfer of interests in intellectual property.

Copyrights

A **copyright** protects the *expression* of a creative work, such as the work of an author, artist, or composer. Copyright owners have the exclusive right to reproduce, sell, perform, or display the work. According to Title 17, Sections 302-303 of the U.S. Code, copyrights in materials created on or after January 1, 1978, and owned by the creator of the work last for the life of the creator

TEAMWORK

In small groups, discuss the pros and cons of registering the copyright for intellectual property you create, such as poetry, music, short stories, etc.

plus 70 years. A work created before January 1, 1978, also lasts for the life of the creator plus 70 years. If such a work is not only created before January 1, 1978, but published before December 31, 2002, the copyright will continue to December 31, 2047, at a minimum. After a copyright expires, the work can be used by anyone without cost or first obtaining permission. An author can transfer ownership of the copyright to others.

Copyrighted works can include songs, books, computer programs, and architectural plans. The expression must be *fixed and original*. Fixed means it is expressed in a permanent way others can understand, for example in writing, painting, computer language, or a blueprint. It is the fixed expression, not the idea, that is protected. If you wrote a book about the Civil War, for example, only the way you used the words would be protected.

Copyright protection begins upon the creation of the original work. In most states, a common law copyright protects from the time the work is created until the creator distributes the material beyond her or his immediate associates. At that point, the creator's rights are protected only if the work has been registered with the U.S. Copyright Office. Registration allows the creator to collect damages for *infringement*, which is the unauthorized copying, sale, display, or performance of the work. Registration also allows the creator to license the subject matter for a *royalty*, or a payment, for use of the work.

Not all unauthorized uses of copyrighted works infringe on the copyright. *Fair use*, which is a limited use of copyrighted works, is granted to critics, researchers, and reporters to carry on their trades. The most important factor in determining whether the defense of fair use is available is the economic impact of the use. Another factor is the quantity of the copied material in relation to the size of the copyrighted work. One novelist might quote a paragraph from another novelist's 300-page book. It would be fair use, because it does not injure the first novelist by causing reduced sales of the quoted novel. Also, the paragraph is but a small portion of the original, copyrighted novel. Finally, teachers may use limited portions of copyrighted materials in their classes.

Trademarks and Service Marks

Business firms may acquire property rights known as trademarks. A **trademark** is a word, mark, symbol, or device that identifies a product of a particular manufacturer or merchant. The mark must be unique and identify and distinguish the product. For example, the word "iPod" is a trademark used by Apple Inc., to identify products made by that company. However, descriptive words, such as "MP3," are not trademarks. They are considered generic terms, and any company may use them. A *service mark* is a unique word, mark, or symbol that identifies a service as opposed to a product.

All states and the federal government have trademark registration laws. Registration is not essential, but if a trademark is registered, it is easier to prove ownership. Common law protection lasts forever if a unique trademark establishes the product in the minds of the public and the trademark is used continuously. The originating company loses its exclusive property right to the trademark if either of the following occurs.

DIGITAL MILLENNIUM COPYRIGHT ACT (DMCA)

The Digital Millennium Copyright Act changed the U.S. copyright law by providing a greatly increased measure of protection for holders of copyrighted works. It has two parts. The first part makes it criminal to produce and sell services, devices, or basic technology intended to thwart measures that restrict access to copyrighted works, such as movies, recorded music, videos, and much more. The second part of the statute makes the very act of trying to get around a measure that controls access to copyrighted materials a crime, whether or not actual infringement is involved.

THINK CRITICALLY

Do you think the criminalization of aids to the attempt, and the attempt itself, of getting around control measures is a good idea? Why or why not?

1. The company permits competitors to refer to similar products by the unique trademark.

2. The trademark becomes generally used as a broad descriptive term. For example, several years ago, the Xerox Company noted that people were making statements like, "I'm going to xerox this memo on the IBM copier." To prevent losing the rights to its trademark, the Xerox Company spent millions of dollars in advertising to remind Americans that "Xerox" referred to a particular company with certain standards and values that were reflected in its products. The ad campaign worked and preserved the company's rights in a very lucrative trademark.

Examples of terms that have become generic are "shredded wheat" and "cellophane." Whereas "Levi's," "Scotch Tape," and "Xerox," remain the property of the original owners.

Patents

Granted by the U.S. Patent and Trademark Office, a **patent** is a property right that *excludes* others from making, using, offering for sale, selling, or importing the invention. The life of a new patent is typically good for 20 years from the date on which the application is filed in the United States. Patents are not renewable. However, an inventor will sometimes patent improvements to the original product and thereby extend the practical life of the initial patent.

Generally, in order to receive a patent, the invention must be novel, nonobvious, useful, and operative. *Novel* typically means that no one has ever thought of the product or process before. *Nonobvious* means that it

Photodisc/Getty Images

Why is it often wise to get a patent for a new invention?

Use Your Judgment

The DuPont Chemical Company of Delaware created a new process for the production of methanol. For various reasons, the company elected to keep the process secret instead of filing for a patent. To profit from its discovery, Dupont began construction of a refinery to utilize the process. During the refinery's construction, a low-flying plane was observed making numerous circles over the construction site. Using the identification numbers on the plane, DuPont was able to discover that it contained photographers who had taken numerous pictures for an undisclosed client. Believing the photos would reveal its trade secret by the layout of the plant and the devices being installed, DuPont has filed suit against the photographers to discover the identity of their client. Once discovered, DuPont plans to sue the client for misappropriation of the trade secret.

THINK CRITICALLY
Do you think DuPont has a right to obtain the identity of the client? Why or why not?

was above the engineering standards in use in the field at the time of creation. *Useful* means that the product or process can be of beneficial use to society. *Operative* means that the device sought to be patented must work to perform the intended purpose. Patents are also given for original designs, original processes, and for new and distinct varieties of plants and other biological creations. According to case law, laws of nature, physical phenomena, and abstract ideas are not patentable subject matter. Like copyrights, patents can be transferred to others.

Trade Secrets

Sometimes a business firm will have important ideas or knowledge that cannot be copyrighted or patented. These ideas can be protected as trade secrets. A **trade secret** is commercially valuable information that the owner attempts to keep secret. If an employee leaves a company and sells a secret formula, process, or customer list, the former employee and the buyer of the trade secret will be liable to the former employer. Typically, trade secrets have no set time limit. They exist as long as the owner makes an effort to protect them.

CheckPOINT

List three situations in which fair use protects the user of materials copyrighted by another.

_____

_____

Think Critically

1. How is copyright law threatened by the photocopier, recordable CDs, the Internet, and cheap data storage devices? Do you think this is a problem that should be corrected? Why or why not?

_____

_____

_____

_____

2. Under what circumstances would you think a business would consider utilizing the trade secret laws instead of patenting its important ideas or knowledge?

_____

_____

_____

_____

3. Could your instructor copyright a test she created for this chapter of your textbook? Could your father copyright a letter he wrote to you at camp? Why or why not?

_____

_____

_____

_____

4. Should patents be issued for genetic engineering that results in new and improved plants or other useful biological combinations? Why or why not?

_____

_____

_____

_____

_____

Make Academic Connections

5. **Sociology** Write an opinion paper on the following question. Which type of intellectual property rights is most important to society? Why?

6. **Research** Search the Internet to determine how many patents are issued each year by the U.S. Patent and Trademark Office. Find five examples of new patents issued and describe them.

Chapter Summary

3.1 Introduction to Property

A. Property is best defined as the rights and interests in things that society allows individuals to claim. Property is commonly categorized as real property or personal property.

B. Property may be acquired by contract, gift, inheritance, adverse possession, eminent domain, dedication, accession, creation, or finding lost property.

3.2 Real Property

A. Real property is comprised of land, buildings, and fixtures. The rights and interests in real property are gathered into a variety of bundles called estates.

B. Restrictions on the use of real property include restrictive covenants, variances, easements, and licenses.

3.3 Bailments

A. A bailment is the temporary transfer of possession and control of personal property subject to an agreement to return it to its owner or to a third party.

B. The three levels of care associated with bailments are extraordinary, ordinary, and minimal.

3.4 Intellectual Property

A. Intellectual property includes copyrights, patents, trademarks, service marks, and trade secrets.

B. The federal and state governments often are involved in protecting intellectual property.

Vocabulary Builder

Choose the term that best fits the definition. Write the letter of the answer in the space provided. Some terms may not be used.

_____ 1. Rights and interest in land, buildings, and fixtures

_____ 2. Bundle of rights in real property received upon taking ownership

_____ 3. Protects the expression of a creative work, such as a song or poem

_____ 4. Commercially valuable information that the owner attempts to keep secret

_____ 5. Word, mark, symbol, or device that identifies a product

_____ 6. All property other than real property

_____ 7. Document by which rights and interests in real property are transferred

_____ 8. A contractual obligation taken on by one party to indemnify the loss incurred by another party

a. bailment
b. copyright
c. deed
d. estate
e. fungible
f. insurance
g. intellectual property
h. patent
i. personal property
j. property
k. real property
l. trademark
m. trade secret

Review Concepts

Point Your
Browser
www.cengage.com/
school/business/21biz

9. Define property.

10. Name five ways to acquire real property.

11. Name the two most common forms of co-ownership of property. Give the attributes of each.

12. What impact on a bailment does the fact that the subject matter is a fungible good have?

13. What are the different types of deeds? What are the features of each?

14. Explain how restrictive covenants, easements, and licenses limit real property rights.

15. What is a bailment, and how do bailments benefit society?

16. What is the difference between an actual and a constructive bailment?

Apply What You Learned

17. A doctor in the United States has invented a cure for cancer. However, she refuses to reveal it, claiming it is her property alone. Is she correct? Explain.

_____

_____

_____

_____

_____

18. Native Americans had a much different concept of property than did the Europeans who settled in the United States. Native Americans did not believe that land could be owned. In your estimation, do we have a better quality of life than the Native Americans did two centuries ago? Why or why not?

_____

_____

_____

_____

_____

19. Anton is a cage fighter who has a very rare blood type. To be prepared in case he needs blood in the future, he regularly goes to a blood bank and gives blood to be held for him in the event of an emergency? Is this a bailment? Why or why not?

_____

_____

_____

_____

_____

20. You hold a patent and are manufacturing the invention it covers. After a year of profitable operation, you discover that a firm in another state is manufacturing a good that seems to infringe on your patent. Your patent attorney advises you that in 50 percent of infringement suits, the patent in dispute is declared invalid. Would you sue? Why or why not?

_____

_____

_____

_____

_____

Make Academic Connections

21. **Environment** Businesses regularly rent out canoes and rafts for float trips on streams. The renters often dump their trash in the water, either accidentally or intentionally. Also, because there are no restroom facilities along many of the waterways, human waste often makes its way into the water. Contact such businesses and ask what precautions, contractual and otherwise, they take to prevent and/or clean up such spoilage. Record their responses below.

_____

_____

_____

_____

22. **Problem Solving** How would you assign responsibility for the clean-up of the spoilage mentioned in Problem 21? By what legal devices would you enforce this responsibility? Prepare a class presentation of your findings for Problems 21 and 22.

23. **Marketing** Search for business advertisements placed by companies offering their expertise to inventors needing to patent and develop their ideas. Ask for sample copies of their contracts and compare and contrast their terms. Write a one-page report describing your observations.

24. **Business Law** Many American freedoms center on the use of property. Consider the various rights covered in the Bill of Rights and record these freedoms on a spreadsheet. Identify what and how property ownership is necessary to enjoy each.

Ethical Dilemma

25. A large university needs land for another parking lot. It begins the process of eminent domain to secure the land. The area it intends to condemn is now an older neighborhood populated mostly by retired couples. The university agrees to pay these people 125 percent of the appraised value of their properties. Is this adequate compensation? What ethical issues are involved in eminent domain cases?

_____

_____

_____

_____

_____

_____

CHAPTER 4

Employment Law

4.1 Agency

4.2 Employer-Employee Relations

4.3 Employment Regulations

Careers in Business Law

arketing

RE/MAX REALTY

RE/MAX Realty was founded in 1973 by Dave and Gail Linger. At the time, commission earned on a home sale by an agent was split 50 percent with the brokerage firm in exchange for office space and support services. This arrangement meant that the top producers paid in the most and supported the part-time, low-producing agents. As a consequence, the residential real estate industry had a high turnover rate. The Lingers changed all that by offering maximum compensation, sophisticated support from permanent staff, and the latitude necessary for success. RE/MAX expanded quickly and now has over 120,000 agents throughout the United States and 65 other countries.

A real estate agent needs strong communication and math skills and a good background in law, especially contract and real estate law. A college degree is not required, but an agent must pass stringent testing to acquire a license. Various classes are offered by the industry to help agents pass the licensing exams.

Think Critically

1. Why must real estate agents be licensed?
2. What are the advantages of working with a professional real estate agent?

PROJECT | Employment Questionnaire

Project Objectives

- Create a questionnaire to understand the use of agency, employment, and independent contracting by local businesses
- Learn how state and federal laws affect employment relationships

©Rob Marmion, 2009/ Used under license from Shutterstock.com

Getting Started

Read the Project Process below. Make a list of any materials you will need.

- Decide how to put the information gathered into an easy-to-read format.
- Go through the *Yellow Pages* for your community. Make a list of ten different types of businesses advertised there. Pick one or more examples of each type of business.

Project Process

4.1 Develop a questionnaire to send to each type of business on your list. In the first section, ask whether the business uses agents and independent contractors, and if so, how? Find out if cost is a factor.

4.2 In the second section of the questionnaire, write questions to learn about the company's employees and employee policies. How many employees does the company have? How many are full-time? Part-time? How does the company go about terminating employees?

4.3 In the third section, ask questions about how state and federal laws affect the company's employment decisions. In addition, investigate how various social insurance programs affect the employment environment.

Chapter Review

Project Wrap-up   Send the questionnaire to at least ten human resources directors of your listed businesses. Compile and analyze the results.

Digital Vision/Getty Images

GOALS

Define agency and explain how and why agencies are created

Compare agents' and principals' duties and authority

Describe how agencies can be terminated

KEY TERMS

agency, p. 94

power of attorney, p. 95

 JUMP START

Susan's dad, knowing that she has a great deal of expertise in computer programming, asks her to contract on his behalf with a group of professional programmers for the building of a website for his startup business. Susan negotiates a very favorable contract for her dad. Later realizing that they have entered into a very unprofitable contract, the would-be web designers seek to avoid it because Susan is a minor. Can they? Why or why not?

Comstock Images/Jupiter Images

Creation of Agency

When two parties establish a relationship in which one may legally bind the other by words or actions, an **agency** is created. The person authorizing another to act in her or his place is called the *principal*. The person authorized is termed the *agent*. An agent acts within the power granted by the principal. This is called the agent's *scope of authority*. As long as the agent acts within the scope of authority, the principal is bound by any deals the agent negotiates with third parties on the principal's behalf.

Agency versus Similar Relationships

To understand agency, you must first understand similar relationships, such as those between employer and employee and between an individual and an independent contractor hired for a project.

Principal-Agent and Employer-Employee Relationships The *principal-agent relationship* is distinguished from a typical *employer-employee relationship* on the basis of the extent and type of control exercised. First, an agent can enter into contracts on behalf of the principal. For example, an insurance agent can enter into a contract on behalf of the insurer with the insured. The typical employee cannot enter contracts on behalf of the employer. For example, an assembly line worker for General Motors does not have the authority to enter into a contract on behalf of her employer. If an employee is granted the power to contract on the employer's behalf, that employee becomes an agent of the employer. The employer is then liable for the agreements that the employee makes on the employer's behalf.

Second, an employer can direct the on-the-job physical actions of the employee. For example, a landscaper can direct his employee as to where to place various plants and how to initially fertilize and water them. A principal does not have the equivalent power over her or his agent. If the principal contracts for this power as well, the agent becomes an employee in the eyes of the law. In such a case, the principal can then, like any other employer, be held liable for the harm caused by the agent in the conduct of employment duties. For example, if the owner of an apartment building hires a real estate agent to rent the units and directs that agent to also clean each unit in preparation for rental, the agent becomes an employee while conducting the cleaning. If he leaves a liquid spill on the kitchen floor from the cleaning and a would-be renter viewing the property slips and falls as a consequence, the employer/owner will be liable for any harm to the prospective renter as a result of the employment relationship.

Independent Contractor An *independent contractor* is neither an agent nor an employee. Independent contractors agree only to provide a result. They do not act to bind another to legal agreements. Neither do they act under the control of another. Whoever hires the independent contractor is not liable for damages caused by the independent contractor's actions. For example, a mason selected by the general contractor to install a brick wall around a building under construction would be an independent contractor.

Authority and Agency

An agency may be created by a principal's express grants of authority. It may also be created by implication from the nature of the two parties' relationship. The circumstances may suggest that an agent has authority. If so, the principal is bound to the contractual obligations that result.

Express Authority An express grant of authority means that the terms are spelled out clearly for both parties. Express authority can be made either orally or in writing. A written agency authorization is called a **power of attorney**. A *general power of attorney* allows the agent to do anything legally necessary to conduct the principal's affairs. A *limited power of attorney* allows the agent to carry out only specific transactions. It also may act to limit the agent to a set period of time.

Implied Authority Whether in writing or stated orally, an express grant of authority to an agent carries with it implied authority to do whatever is reasonably necessary to carry out the specified transaction(s).

Apparent Authority If the principal creates in another person the appearance of authority, the courts often will hold that the person had apparent authority to enter into contracts on the other's behalf. For example, if a store manager introduced a new, untrained employee to a prospective customer as a sales agent who "would be able to help him with his purchase," the store would likely be bound by a contract entered into on its behalf by that employee. In addition, if an unauthorized act is *ratified* (approved by accepting the benefits of the unauthorized act), the ratifying party can be bound as a principal.

Minors If a minor becomes a principal in an agency relationship, that minor retains the power to avoid any contracts entered into on his or her behalf. In addition, the minor can avoid the agency contract itself. However, a person without contractual capacity, such as a minor, can be an agent. The adult who makes a contract through a minor agent cannot avoid the contract on that ground.

CheckPOINT

What is the difference between an independent contractor and an agent?

_____

_____

Duties of the Agent and the Principal

Once an agency has been established, each party to the agency has distinct duties to the other.

Duties of the Principal to the Agent

The principal has the following four duties. All of these duties except the requirement of good faith are subject to revision or elimination by means of the agency contract.

Duty to Compensate the Agent The principal must pay for the agent's services if this is required under the agency contract. If such payment is not required, the arrangement is referred to as a *gratuitous agency*.

Duty to Reimburse the Agent An agency contract may require that the agent's own funds be used to carry out the duties of the contract. If so, the principal is obligated to reimburse the agent for those expenses.

Duty to Pay for the Agent's Liabilities to Third Parties In properly carrying out agency duties, the agent may incur contractual or other liability through no fault of his or her own. If this happens, the principal has an implied duty to make good the agent's loss.

Duty to Adhere in Good Faith to the Agency Contract The principal must comply with the agency's terms openly and honestly. The agent's ability to carry out her or his duties must not be hindered by the principal.

Duties of the Agent to the Principal

The agent has the following four duties.

Duty to Be Obedient An agent is responsible for obeying the lawful directions of the principal. The principal may recover from the agent any damages that result from the agent's failure to obey.

Duty to Be Loyal to the Principal The agent is held to the duty to act loyally toward the principal. If the agent's personal interests are affected by a transaction for the principal, the agent must inform the principal that this is the case. The agency's business must not be conducted with friends, relatives, or businesses of the agent without the principal's prior approval.

Duty to Keep Agency Funds and Property Separate The agent must keep agency funds and other property separate from her or his own personal resources. The agent also must be prepared to account for all agency funds and other property under his or her control. If the agent mixes personal and agency property in a way that makes it impossible to distinguish or separate it, the principal can claim all of the property.

Duty to Use Reasonable Care and Skill When carrying out the principal's directions, the agent must exercise reasonable care and skill. If the agent fails to do so, he or she may be held liable.

©AVAVA, 2009/ Used under license from Shutterstock.com

Why is it important for an agent to keep agency funds separate from personal funds?

CheckPOINT

What are the duties of the agent to the principal?

_____

_____

What actions or events may end an agency?

Termination of Agencies

Generally, both the agent and the principal have the power, but not the right, to terminate the agency at any time. This means that either may end the agency relationship whether or not they are legally justified in doing so. However, if they are not so justified, the person who terminates must compensate the other by paying damages. Typically, the principal terminates by revoking the agent's authority and notifying appropriate parties of the action. The agent usually terminates by ceasing to work on the principal's behalf under the contract.

Gratuitous Agency

As previously mentioned, a gratuitous agency exists when the agent receives no payment. Usually, a gratuitous agent cannot recover any damages if the authority is revoked. Likewise, a principal normally cannot recover any damages from a gratuitous agent who abandons the agency.

Agreement

An ordinary agency expires at the time provided in the contract that created it. This may be defined as a particular length of time, the occurrence of an event, or the completion of certain tasks. If no time is stated in the agency contract, the agency continues for a reasonable time. An agency can be ended at any time if both the principal and agent agree to terminate it.

Operation of Law

An agency ordinarily is terminated upon the death, insanity, or bankruptcy of the principal or the agent. Also, if it becomes impossible to perform the agency, it is ended. This may happen if the subject matter of the agency is destroyed or if a change of law makes the agent's required actions illegal.

Notice of Termination

Except where the agency is discharged as a matter of law, the principal has the duty to give notice of its termination. This notice must be given to parties with whom the agent has had prior dealings for the principal. If the principal fails to give adequate notice, he or she is liable on contracts negotiated by the former agent with such parties.

CheckPOINT

Why must the principal give notice of the agency termination?

_____

_____

Think Critically

1. Under what circumstances might you utilize an agency? How would you select your agent?

   _____

   _____

   _____

2. You are planning to take a two-month vacation. You will be completely inaccessible during that time. What sort of general and limited powers of attorney might you want to set up before leaving?

   _____

   _____

   _____

3. Give examples of when an agent might become obligated to spend his or her own funds to carry out the duties of an agency. How could reimbursement be arranged in each circumstance?

   _____

   _____

4. What does it mean to say that the agent and principal have the power but not the right to terminate the agency?

   _____

   _____

   _____

Make Academic Connections

5. **Communication** Write a limited power of attorney that provides for an agent to take care of your mother, who is in a nursing home, while you are away for a year.

6. **Sports and Entertainment Law** Identify and contact agents for sports figures and actors. Ask them for copies of their standard agency contracts. Compare and contrast these contracts. Develop explanations for the differences you find. Present your findings in class.

7. **Geography** Contact the embassy or trade envoy of another country. Ask what powers it has to act on behalf of industries in its home country. Can it negotiate contracts, arrange for visits by trade representatives, provide information on the businesses in its country, or give samples of the products involved? Write a one-page report on your findings.

GOALS

Describe the terms of employment contracts

Explain the legal rights and duties involved in the employer-employee relationship, including termination of the employment contract

KEY TERMS

employment, p. 100

fringe benefits, p. 101

terminable at will, p. 101

 JUMP START

Andy Pullet worked for Crowson's Fried Chicken in Columbia, Missouri, for three years. Within a month after he left its employment, he started his own fried chicken restaurant using Crowson's recipes and the cooking and serving processes he learned there. Crowson's promptly filed suit, asking the court to enforce the noncompete clause in Andy's employment contract. The contract term read, "I will not compete with Crowson's for a period of three years after leaving its employ or within a ten-mile radius of any of its stores." How should the court treat the agreement?

Photodisc/Getty Images

Legal Aspects of Employment

Why is the study of employment so important? The answer is simple. Without that relationship, most of the productive work in our society would not get done. If we want to be properly fed, clothed, and housed, employment is crucial to us. The study of employment also is important because of the many detailed regulations that affect the employer-employee relationship.

Employment is defined simply as a relationship in which the *employer* pays the *employee* to do work under the control and direction of the employer. The detailed terms of this relationship are found in the employment contract. Employment contracts typically involve written, oral, and implied terms. Like any other agreement, an employment contract must contain all of the essential elements of a contract in order to be enforceable. Terms such as compensation and fringe benefits are typically expressly agreed upon, as may be the job's duration or the length of advance notice required in the event of termination.

Implied terms, such as whether or not the worker should provide for his own safety gear, may be taken from the established practice on the job site. In addition, compliance with state and federal regulations pertaining to the employment situation, such as the withholding of social security taxes from an employee's pay, are treated as being implied by law.

Typically, a failure to follow the express terms of an employment contract will be treated as a breach that will bring about the termination of the employer-employee contractual relationship.

CheckPOINT

Define employment.

_____

_____

Duties of Employers and Employees

Generally, detailed governmental regulation of the work environment began as part of the response to the Great Depression of the 1930's. Before that, common law had created legal standards for participants in the employment relationship. Those standards are still valid today but have been augmented by rules and regulations set down by federal and state agencies. The common law standards usually are stated in terms of the duties that the participants owe to each other. They are in addition to the duties expressed in an oral or written employment contract. Most of them parallel the duties related to agency law.

Duties of the Employer

The employer has three duties to employees. These include the duty to compensate, the duty to specify a reasonable range of tasks, and the duty to provide a proper work environment.

Compensation The employer's primary duty to the employee is to compensate the employee for her or his productive efforts. This is done principally by paying a salary or wages. Compensation also can include **fringe benefits**, which are forms of payment not directly related to work performance. Fringe benefits may include pensions, vacation time, and health insurance. As long as the employee shows himself or herself ready, willing, and able to perform during the fixed period, the compensation is due whether or not any work was performed.

Unless they specify a definite term or require notice beforehand, many employment contracts are **terminable at will**. Either party can end such at-will relationships without notice at any time without involving the courts.

Reasonable Range of Duties and Treatment The employer has a duty to the employee to properly specify a reasonable range of tasks to be completed.

TEAMWORK

In small groups, discuss the value of fringe benefits to employees. Which fringe benefits do you think are most valuable to employees, and why?

©Bobby Deal/RealDealPhoto, 2009/ Used under license from Shutterstock.com

What is meant by the employer's duty to provide a "reasonable range of duties and treatment"?

The employer also must treat the employee properly as he or she performs them.

The employee cannot be required to perform acts outside the scope of the job as defined in the employment contract. Such requests would provide the employee with adequate legal grounds to justify termination of the employment relationship. However, quitting a job merely because the treatment is harsher than expected or the tasks are more difficult is not legally defensible.

The employer is not permitted to subject the employee to unreasonably harsh treatment, such as assaults or batteries. For example, if the employer beats the employee, the employee can quit without any fear of liability for breach of contract.

Proper Work Environment An employee does not have control over the details of how the work is done. Therefore, the law maintains that she or he is entitled to a safe work environment. Unsafe working conditions provide the employee with another justification for ending the employment relationship without liability for breach of contract.

Duties of the Employee

Many of the employee's duties, such as obedience, loyalty, and reasonable care and skill, find their basis in agency law. However, the duty of providing production in return for compensation is at the heart of the exchange that exists in all employment relationships. This duty is not found in all agencies.

Production The primary duty of any employee is to produce a satisfactory work product. Work that is below standard in either quality or quantity can result in justifiable discharge of the employee.

Obedience Implicit in the employment relationship is the employee's agreement to submit to the detailed control and direction of the employer. This detailed oversight is what distinguishes the employment relationship from that involving the independent contractor or agent. The employee must obey the lawful orders and rules of the employer that fall within the scope of employment. Failing to do so provides grounds for dismissal.

Loyalty In return for compensation, the employer buys not only obedience but an expectation of loyalty as well. Loyalty does not extend beyond the job, however. An employer may expect that its employee will not reveal confidential information or otherwise do harm to its business. However, the employer cannot demand that the employee use its products in his or her private life.

Reasonable Care and Skill By entering into an employment contract, the employee implies that she or he has the skills needed to perform the job properly and with the proper care. If experience shows that this is not the

Why are employees expected to show reasonable care and skill?

case, the employer is justified in discharging the employee. The exception to this is an employee hired to take part in a training program.

One of the main reasons for the employer to discharge an improperly qualified employee is the potential liability if such an employee injures someone or something while acting within the scope of employment. In such a situation, the employer can be held vicariously liable for the harm done. *Vicarious liability* is a legal doctrine that imposes responsibility on one party for the actionable conduct of another party based on an existing relationship between the two parties.

The rule of law that places vicarious liability on the employer or principal is known as *respondeat superior*. This is a Latin term which translates to "let the master answer." This rule allows an injured party to hold the employee and the employer jointly liable for the harm done by the former. The justification for the rule lies in the high degree of control that the employer exercises over the employee. As long as the employee acts within the scope of employment, the detailed training and directives given by the employer make the employer accountable for the employee's harmful actions.

Criminal acts generally remain the sole responsibility of the employee. Unless the employer has specifically authorized the crime, the criminal intent of the employer cannot be inferred from the employee's acts. There are exceptions to this rule. The most glaring is the criminal responsibility placed on the employers of those who, even against their employers' directions, sell impure foods or alcoholic beverages to minors or to persons too intoxicated to drive.

Termination of the Employment Contract

The general rule regarding termination of the employment relationship is that it can be ended at any time by any party to it for practically any reason. This is the "at-will" termination mentioned earlier. Such terminations do not ordinarily

Tech Literacy

CYBERSLACKING

Computers and the Internet have greatly increased productivity in the workplace. However, these important tools also have presented temptation that some workers cannot resist. This phenomenon, called "cyberslacking," is widespread in the U.S. workplace. A recent Vault.com survey found that 90 percent of U.S. workers say they have surfed nonwork-related Internet sites during office hours. Eighty-four percent say they have sent personal e-mail from work. A 2008 study, however, argued that allowing employees short personal breaks in the form of e-mails or Internet gaming is actually beneficial to work productivity and creative thinking.

THINK CRITICALLY

Which, if any, of the duties employees owe to their employers do you think cyberslacking violates? Justify your answer.

create a basis for a lawsuit, unless a contract or a collective bargaining agreement has set standards for dismissal.

Exceptions to At-Will Termination There are exceptions to the "at-will" rule. A few states require that firings be made as a result of good faith evaluations of the various factors involved in employment. Other states protect employees who are fired for refusing to violate the law or for refusing to waive their rights under certain laws, such as workers' compensation. Most states, though, still follow the at-will perspective. The federal government has legislated exceptions in favor of *whistleblowers*. These are employees who alert the authorities to the misconduct of their employer. This applies even when the federal government is the employer.

Noncompete Clauses Employers who must utilize secret information on product formulas or vital processes often have *agreements not to compete*, commonly called noncompete clauses, in their employment contracts. Such agreements limit the ability of a worker to enter into competition with his or her former employer for a reasonable period after termination of the employment relationship. If written too broadly, agreements of this kind counteract federal laws intended to spur competition. The courts will either void such agreements or reduce them to reasonable proportions. Generally, the legal effectiveness of such agreements extends to two years after leaving the employer and applies only within the market region of the ex-employer.

CheckPOINT

What is "at-will" termination?

_____

_____

Think Critically

1. What are the advantages of being the employer in the employment relationship? What are the advantages of being an employee? Which would you choose?

2. In a terminable at-will employment relationship, could an employee quit because she had a better job offer? Could an employer fire someone because he smoked? Why or why not in each case?

3. What is the basis for holding employers vicariously liable?

4. Would you want to stay at a job where you had "blown the whistle" over some improper conduct? Why or why not?

Make Academic Connections

5. **Ecology** Search the Internet for articles about whistleblowers in the area of hazardous waste. Has the legal protection afforded these whistleblowers been adequate? Could you devise a better scheme of protection?

6. **History** Research the history of the minimum wage law as a part of the U.S. Fair Labor Standards Act. What factors motivated the passage of this law? What factors typically cause an increase in the minimum wage? Has the law been effective in promoting prosperity for those at the bottom of the wage scale? Has the law had unintended consequences?

GOALS

Discuss the laws and programs that regulate employment

Describe the regulations for employment contracts

Describe regulations involving job safety and employees who can't work

Recognize the social insurance programs that indirectly affect the work environment

KEY TERMS

discrimination in employment, p. 107

labor union, p. 110

collective bargaining, p. 110

unfair labor practices, p. 110

boycott, p. 110

unemployment compensation, p. 114

 JUMP START

Jack Elzee retired from teaching when he was in his mid-50's after a 25-year career at a state university. Three years later, he decided to re-enter the job market and applied for a position at a nearby private college. Jack was one of two candidates. The other candidate was a 30-year-old, part-time instructor. Both of the candidates presented their credentials to the departmental faculty. Jack mentioned his teaching awards and high student evaluations, his 17 authored books in the field, and numerous published papers. The other candidate had published two articles in a regional journal. Two weeks later, Jack received a letter notifying him that the other candidate had been selected for the position by faculty vote. Jack decided to investigate. He discovered that the vote was made based on the faculty's question, "Which candidate has the greatest long-term potential for the college?" He also learned that the other candidate's in-laws were long-time contributors to the college. What recourse might Jack have against the college under discrimination laws? Explain.

Digital Vision/Getty Images

Government Involvement

The government often has to become involved in employment relationships. Usually this involvement is through the actions of various state and federal boards and agencies. These governmental bodies play a role in four major areas of the employment relationship.

1. The government tries to see that all job applicants are given equal opportunity to win the position pursued by insuring they are evaluated solely on their ability to do the job and without any improper discrimination.

2. The government oversees the bargaining that leads to major employment contracts around the country.

3. The government seeks to insure proper working conditions and treatment of those who are injured on the job.

4. The government provides supplemental assistance to those encountering problems indirectly related to the work environment. "Social insurance" programs benefit the retired, the unemployed, the disabled, those with extraordinary health problems, and the dependents of deceased wage earners.

Equal Employment Opportunity Commission

In 1964, Congress passed the Civil Rights Act, which established the Equal Employment Opportunity Commission (EEOC). The EEOC was authorized to utilize lawsuits and mediation to fight against discrimination in employment.

Title VII of the Civil Rights Act makes discrimination in employment illegal. Title VII defines **discrimination in employment** as hiring, promoting, or discharging on the basis of race, color, sex, religion, or national origin. Amendments to the Civil Rights Act gave the EEOC power to force some employers and all unions, employment agencies, and other entities to eliminate improper discrimination. Employers subject to EEOC laws are those who have more than 15 employees for each working day in each of 20 or more calendar weeks in the current or preceding calendar year and whose business has an impact on interstate commerce. The EEOC also can act against seemingly neutral rules that have an improper impact. An example is requiring security guards to be at least six feet tall and to weigh at least 200 pounds. This requirement would likely produce an all-male security force.

Disabled Employees

The federal Rehabilitation Act of 1973 adds disability to the categories of prohibited discriminatory bases. As interpreted by current case law, the Rehabilitation Act as amended in 1990 prohibits discrimination in hiring, promoting, and firing based on disability by public and private "entities" (not merely employers) that receive federal assistance.

The Americans with Disabilities Act (ADA) goes beyond merely prohibiting discrimination based on disability by prescribing what an employer must do for its disabled employees. Under the ADA, an employer must provide "reasonable accommodations" for a qualified worker who happens to have a substantial physical or mental impairment. What accommodations are reasonable varies with the nature and cost of the impairment and the work requirements. The impairment can be the result of a disease or an accident. The accommodations can include visual aids, hearing aids, or changes in ventilation, lighting, and other elements of the work environment.

Another related law, the Pregnancy Discrimination Act, pertains to pregnancy, giving birth, and the recovery from delivery. It requires that an employer treat these conditions in the same manner in which it treats other physical problems producing an inability to work.

Age Discrimination

A similar law enforced by the EEOC is the Age Discrimination in Employment Act. This federal law, passed in 1967, makes it illegal for private employers to discriminate against persons because they are age 40 or over. In addition to prohibiting age discrimination in hiring, firing, promotion, or pay, the act prohibits advertising for job applicants in terms that suggest a preference for youth or for persons in a particular age bracket. Even advertising a desire for a "recent graduate" is improper.

Sexual Harassment

The EEOC regulations covering sexual harassment in the workplace require the elimination of harassing sexual advances, requests for sexual favors, and other verbal or physical abuse of a sexual nature. Although this regulation applies throughout employment, the protection is especially necessary during the job application process. When sexual harassment comes from a supervisor, the employer is strictly liable for the improper conduct. When it comes from coworkers, the employer is liable only if the supervisor knows or should have known of the conduct and has not taken effective action to eliminate it.

Bona Fide Occupational Qualifications

Exceptions may be made in some of the discriminatory categories mentioned above. These exceptions typically fall under what are termed *bona fide occupational qualifications* (BFOQs). These BFOQs allow types of discrimination that are reasonably necessary to the conduct of a specific business. Here, what is "reasonable" is the issue. Is it reasonable to have only Baptists as faculty members at a Baptist college? Is it reasonable to have only men as guards in an all-male maximum-security prison? The answers vary dramatically from person to person, interest group to interest group, government entity to government entity, political party to political party, time to time, and within the legal system.

Affirmative Action Plans

One of the most controversial areas in discrimination law involves *affirmative action plans*. Such plans are "voluntarily" created by employers according to EEOC guidelines. The plans set down methods and time frames for actions to eliminate the *adverse impact*, or unfavorable effect, of an employer's past discrimination on certain subgroups, such as women and racial minorities. Percentages are used as general guidelines to determine whether or not an adverse impact exists. Individuals in the adversely impacted subgroups may then be hired or promoted ahead of similarly or better-qualified employees to achieve a satisfactory balance. Such actions often lead employees who were passed over to make charges of *reverse discrimination*. The actions may also lead to the use of *quotas*. This is the setting aside of a certain number of positions to be filled only by a previously adversely affected subgroup.

Anton Mllesevec had worked for 16 years as a machinist in his country of origin. After migrating to the United States and working as a dishwasher in a Miami restaurant for three years, he applied for a job at a local machine shop. As he and his American born nephew, Hariste, walked in the door of the shop, he noticed a sign that read "English Only." Even after three years of living in America, Anton's ability to speak English was poor, so he had brought his nephew along to translate for him. With his nephew's help, he filled out the employment application. The shop's manager then asked Anton to take the standard test given to all applicants to determine his ability to perform as a machinist. The manager motioned to the other 16 applicants and said that they had passed the test. Anton was then given a plan for a large gear to be produced on the shop's equipment. The specifications, including the material to be used and the dimensions of the gear, were written in English but not in numbers. When Anton asked to have Hariste translate, the shop's owner said "no" because Hariste would not be with Anton on the job. Anton had made many similar gears, but he did not pass the test as a result of being unable to read the plan.

THINK CRITICALLY

If you were Anton's lawyer in an EEOC discrimination hearing, which part of Title VII would you allege the machine shop violated by its requirement of English only? What would be the shop's defense(s)?

Individuals Prohibited from Working

While some laws encourage proper employment practices, others prohibit employment. For example, certain federal and state laws make it illegal to employ individuals who are 13 years old or younger. However, exemptions are granted to certain occupations for minors. For example, minors 13 and under can be employed to act, deliver newspapers, and work on farms, as long as the work is not hazardous. Between the ages of 14 and 16, minors also can be employed as office workers and gas station attendants. They may not work in factories, around machines, or in hazardous work areas.

TEAMWORK

Review the help-wanted ads in the newspaper. Can you find examples of discriminatory practices in the way the ads are phrased?

CheckPOINT

How does Title VII of the Civil Rights Act define discrimination in employment?

_____

_____

Employment Contract Negotiations

The government oversees the bargaining that leads to major employment contracts around the country.

National Labor Relations Act

In 1935, the National Labor Relations Act (NLRA) was passed by Congress. The NLRA created a system of regulation that assures fairness and order in the process of negotiating employment contracts. It set up procedures for employees to select a representative organization to bargain on their behalf with their employers. This representative is typically known as a **labor union**. The negotiations over conditions and terms of employment between representatives of a work force and its employer are known as **collective bargaining**.

The NLRA also made certain activities on the part of a union or an employer illegal. These activities are referred to as **unfair labor practices**. The National Labor Relations Board (NLRB) investigates and makes determinations on complaints of unfair labor practices. They include the refusal to participate in collective bargaining, firings, intimidation of workers, and boycotts aimed at those who do business with an employer. A **boycott** is a refusal to do business with a particular person or firm in order to obtain concessions (employee-favorable alterations in pay or working conditions). A *secondary boycott* involves causing third parties to agree to cease doing business with a firm with which a union is involved in a dispute.

The NLRA requires unions to give notice of their intent to strike. A *strike* is a collective work stoppage by employees to pressure the employer to give in to union demands.

The NLRA allows employers freedom of speech to comment on unionization. Finally, individual states have been given the right to pass *right-to-work laws* that prohibit collective bargaining agreements from requiring union membership as a condition of employment.

Fair Labor Standards Act

The Fair Labor Standards Act (FLSA), passed in 1938, sets hours and wage guidelines for any person who works in or produces goods for interstate commerce. Many state laws copy these guidelines and make them applicable to persons not covered under the FLSA. Under the FLSA, no covered worker can be employed for more than 40 hours a week without being paid time-and-a-half for overtime. In addition, the FLSA also sets the lowest amount that can be paid for hourly wages, called the *minimum wage*. Note that the FLSA hours and wage standards are subject to numerous exemptions.

Equal Pay Act of 1963

Similarly, the EEOC enforces the Equal Pay Act of 1963. This makes it illegal to use gender as a basis for paying one worker less than another who is performing similar work. The opportunity for all aspects of compensation, from overtime to pensions, must be equal for men and women doing jobs that are performed under similar working conditions and that require the same level of effort, skill, and responsibility.

CheckPOINT

What do right-to-work laws prohibit?

_____

_____

Regulations on Job Safety and Employees Who Can't Work

Two more areas of government regulation pertain to the quality and safety of the job environment and to employees who cannot work. Employees may not be able to work due to family medical conditions or injuries on the job.

Job Safety Regulations

In 1970, Congress created the *Occupational Safety and Health Administration* (OSHA). OSHA's purpose is to establish and enforce federal health and safety standards in the workplace. Employees have the right to request an OSHA inspection if they suspect a violation of an OSHA rule or regulation. If the inspection reveals such a violation, the employer will be cited and required to appear at a hearing to defend against being penalized. OSHA inspectors conducting an investigation are required to have search warrants if they do not receive the employer's voluntary consent for inspection.

Absences Due to Family Medical Conditions

Another federal statute, the Family and Medical Leave Act (FAMLA), sets down rules for employers whose employees are unable to work because of serious medical conditions. FAMLA rules apply to employers in businesses with 50 or more employees. Covered employers must grant an eligible employee up to a total of 12 workweeks of unpaid leave during any 12-month period. Allowable absences include giving birth, attending to the care of a newborn child or an adoptive or foster child, attending to an immediate family member (spouse, child, or parent) with a serious health condition, and recuperating from of a serious medical condition.

In addition, the employer must maintain health insurance on the employee during the leave. The employer also must give the employee the same job or a similar one upon return. In 2008, the provisions of FAMLA were extended to cover military families as well.

©Rafa Irusta, 2009/ Used under license from Shutterstock.com

How does OSHA help keep employees safe?

Cross-Cultural Relationships

UNIONS OF THREE NATIONS FILE COMPLAINTS AGAINST NORTH CAROLINA LAW

As a somewhat unintended consequence of NAFTA (North American Free Trade Agreement), the North American Agreement on Labor Cooperation (NAALC) was reached. It was intended to promote uniformity in labor policies among Mexico, Canada, and the United States. Most significantly, the agreement encourages the right to collective bargaining and the right to strike. Most observers thought that the main application of the Agreement would be to correct the often deplorable labor situation in Mexico. Instead, one of the first major internationally coordinated actions was the filing of complaints in Mexico and Canada by 40 or more unions and trade groups from all three countries against a state law of North Carolina. The North Carolina law prohibits public employees from forming labor associations and striking and has resulted in public employees facing injury and other severe consequences of understaffing.

Think Critically

Should a law passed by North Carolina be able to be negated by actions of courts or agencies in foreign countries? Do you think such internal interference is warranted in this case? Explain your answers.

Absences Due to Injuries on the Job

To assist workers injured on the job, states have passed workers' compensation statutes. These statutes require employers to buy insurance that would pay injured employees benefits regardless of who is responsible for the injury. Such assurance of benefits was given to employees as a substitute for the option of bringing a negligence suit against the employer. These benefits generally cover only medical expenses and a certain percentage of the injured employee's lost wages. If the employee cannot continue in her or his former occupation because of the injury, the system provides for *vocational rehabilitation*, which is training to assume another type of job.

Eligibility Most injuries that fall under the workers' compensation systems are related to the work and occur while the employee is on the job. In the phrasing of the typical state workers' compensation statute, the injury must "arise out of and in the course of the covered employment."

Potential for Lawsuit In certain unusual cases, the employee is not bound by the workers' compensation laws and can pursue suit against the employer. For example, when the employer does not participate in the workers' compensation insurance program even though lawfully required to do so, the employee may bring suit. The employee may also bring suit if the employer has intentionally acted to harm the employee or knowingly permitted conditions that would bring injury to the employee. Finally, suit is allowed where the employee or the injury is not required to be covered by workers' compensation.

CheckPOINT

What time limits are set on unpaid leave eligibility under FAMLA?

_____

_____

Social Insurance

In addition to programs directly related to the work environment, both the state and federal governments provide *social insurance* programs to help protect against the effects of retirement, unemployment, disabilities, extraordinary health problems, and the loss to dependent(s) of a primary wage earner. These programs are generally made available through the provisions of the Social Security Act and are labeled Retirement, Survivors', Disability, and Health Insurance (RSDHI). Unemployment insurance programs are also provided for indirectly under the Act but are controlled and administered by the various states.

Retirement Insurance

Social security taxes are deducted from employees' paychecks. As an employee pays these taxes over time, the worker acquires credits called "quarters." After a set number of quarters have been earned, the worker becomes eligible for various social security programs. The insured may begin collecting partial retirement benefits beginning at the age of 62 but will never be eligible to receive full benefits. If the insured waits until age 65 (or later depending on the worker's birth year), she or he will receive full benefits based on the amount of contributions she or he has made. The benefit amount is tied to the cost of living and subject to periodic review. Note that any Social Security retirement benefit is only meant to be supplemental to a worker's primary retirement plan's payments.

Survivor's Insurance

Another set of benefits under the Social Security Act is available to the survivors of an eligible worker. Among others, these survivor benefits accrue to a widow or widower 60 or older and dependent children under 18 (or 19 if still in high school).

Disability Insurance

Benefits also are extended to those who fall victim to a severe, long-lasting disability that keeps them from doing "any substantial work." The person applying for these benefits must show that the condition causing the physical or mental disability is expected to continue indefinitely or result in death. To be eligible for these benefits, the disabled person must have earned a certain number of credits from work and cannot refuse reasonable medical treatment.

Health Insurance

Social Security Act benefits are also available to cover the costs of medical care necessary for a person to recover his or her physical well-being after an illness. This program, referred to as *Medicare*, is primarily for those 65 or older with enough work credits to be eligible. (Note that the states in conjunction with the federal government offer a program entitled *Medicaid* to those unable to get needed medical services due to low income. The income levels necessary for eligibility in these programs vary from state to state.)

Medicare is divided into two basic programs. The first is for hospital expenses; the second pays for things such as the services of physicians and surgeons, prescription drugs, ambulance charges, and many other expenses related to medical treatment. Unlike the hospital expense program, which is paid for out of the social security tax, the latter program is voluntary and requires the payment of a monthly premium by those enrolled.

What types of health benefits are provided by the Social Security Act?

Unemployment Insurance

Unemployment compensation is money paid to qualified workers who have lost their jobs. Government entities, typically the states in conjunction with the federal government, or private insurance funds pay such compensation to help the discharged worker maintain a standard of living until a new job is found. Eligibility requirements vary from state to state. Generally, however, this compensation is available only to workers who have worked a required number of periods during the last year and have been *discharged without cause*, meaning the loss of the job was not due to improper conduct. Workers who are *discharged for cause,* such as those who quit voluntarily or who are currently taking part in a strike, are not eligible for unemployment compensation. The maximum length of time unemployment benefits are paid is set by the federal government. This time period is usually set at 26 weeks but sometimes extended during harsh economic conditions.

CheckPOINT

What is the difference between Medicare and Medicaid?

_____

_____

Think Critically

1. Why does the government become involved in the employment relationship?

_____

_____

_____

_____

2. What practical effect do right-to-work laws have on unions?

_____

_____

_____

3. Should the period that unemployment benefits are paid be extended indefinitely?

_____

_____

_____

4. Why would vocational rehabilitation be important for employees whose job-related injuries have left them unable to perform that job?

_____

_____

_____

_____

Make Academic Connections

5. **Research** Use the Internet and library resources to discover the history and current status of labor unions around the world. In what countries are unions a viable force in the marketplace? In what countries are there no effective unions? What generalizations can you make from this data?

6. **Math** Research in your local and regional papers and with Department of Labor officials to discover what kind of affirmative action plans have been put into operation in your area. Check the details of these plans to determine what percentages of each subgroup have been required. Check the data from the last census for your area to see how the quota percentages match up to the percentages of each subgroup in the overall population base. Make a spreadsheet to keep track of the information you find. Can you explain the differences?

Chapter Summary

4.1 Agency

A. When two parties establish a relationship whereby one may legally bind the other by words or actions, an agency has been created.

B. Duties of the principal include to compensate and reimburse the agent and to adhere in good faith to the agency contract. The agent has a duty to be obedient and loyal, to keep agency funds and property separate, and to use reasonable care and skill.

4.2 Employer-Employee Relations

A. Employment contracts cover such things as compensation, fringe benefits, duration of employment, and advance notification requirements in the event of termination.

B. An employer's duties are to compensate the employee, to be reasonable in defining the employee's job, and to provide a proper work environment. An employee's duties are to produce a satisfactory work product, obey the employer's lawful rules and regulations, be loyal to the employer, and utilize reasonable care and skill on the job.

4.3 Employment Regulations

A. The government often seeks to intervene in the employment relationship, typically to balance the power of the employer and employee.

B. The government oversees the bargaining that leads to major employment contracts around the country.

C. The government seeks to insure proper working conditions and treatment of those who are injured on the job.

D. Under the provision of the Social Security Act, the government provides supplemental assistance to those who are eligible.

Vocabulary Builder

Choose the term that best fits the definition. Write the letter of the answer in the space provided. Some terms may not be used.

_____ 1. Hiring, promoting, or discharging on the basis of race, color, sex, religion, or national origin

_____ 2. A relationship in which one party can legally bind another party by words or actions

_____ 3. Forms of payment not directly related to work performance

_____ 4. A written agency authorization

_____ 5. The representative that bargains on behalf of the employees in a collective bargaining session

_____ 6. Employment contract that can be ended without notice by either party

_____ 7. A refusal to do business with a particular person or firm in order to obtain concessions

_____ 8. Money paid to qualified workers who have lost their jobs

a. agency

b. boycott

c. collective bargaining

d. discrimination in employment

e. employment

f. fringe benefits

g. labor union

h. power of attorney

i. terminable at will

j. unemployment compensation

k. unfair labor practices

Review Concepts

Point Your
Browser
www.cengage.com/
school/business/21biz

9. Name the two parties in an agency and describe their roles.

_____

_____

_____

10. What are the different types of powers of attorney?

_____

_____

_____

11. Explain the difference between an agent and an employee.

_____

_____

_____

12. Explain the difference between an agent and an independent contractor.

_____

_____

13. What duties does the principal owe to the agent?

_____

_____

_____

14. What duties does an employer owe to his or her employee?

_____

_____

_____

15. What duties does an agent owe to the principal?

_____

_____

_____

16. What duties does an employee owe to his employer?

_____

_____

_____

17. What role does a labor union play in employer-employee relationships?

_____

_____

_____

18. List at least four unfair labor practices.

_____

_____

_____

_____

19. Describe the two basic programs available under the Medicare system?

_____

_____

_____

_____

Apply What You Learned

20. Why are noncompete clauses in employment contracts allowable in some cases?

_____

_____

21. Should secondary boycotts remain illegal? Why or why not?

_____

_____

_____

22. Should an employer who takes reasonable but ineffective action upon being notified of sexual harassment by coworkers be held liable?

_____

_____

23. Why is it important to the consumer to be sure that all forms of job discrimination are prohibited?

_____

_____

24. Why are workers' compensation laws supported by businesses?

_____

_____

25. Why are unemployment benefits not paid to striking workers?

_____

_____

_____

Make Academic Connections

26. **Environment** Are government agents really agents? Find out what sort of latitude the Environmental Protection Agency gives its employees to settle disputes, cite offenders, and prosecute cases. Present your findings in class.

27. **Problem Solving** An employee for a woodworking business gains 375 pounds. He then petitions the government under the ADA to require his employer to install an elevator to allow him access to his workstation. Do you think being obese should be considered a disability? Should the elevator be provided even if the extra cost will hurt the competitiveness of the products? Would your answers be the same if an employee who has smoked all his life has a lung removed and needs the elevator?

28. **Marketing** Watch at least 10 television commercials. Keep a record on a spreadsheet of how many people with disabilities you see in the commercials. Does this fairly reflect the number of disabled people in the general population? Is this a form of discrimination? What federal statute(s) might provide a remedy?

29. **Business Law** Contact a representative of the Mexican government dealing with plant relocation. Find out what kind of laws relating to disability, discrimination, and harassment the government applies to its industries. Write a two-page report summarizing your conclusions.

Ethical Dilemma

30. You are a chemist working in a private laboratory that is under government contract to analyze water samples from around the state. Water samples you analyzed last week at the largest recreational lake in the state show abnormally high levels of E. coli. Several of the samples are 20 to 30 times the allowable EPA limit. The results of your tests are sent to the state's Department of Health. Almost a month later, no action has been taken to warn the public. You know that tourist revenue is crucial to the lake's businesses. Making the report public could result in vacation cancellations and layoffs of hundreds of employees. Should you blow the whistle on the cover-up and risk joining the ranks of those consequently losing their jobs? Why or why not?

_____

_____

_____

_____

_____

_____

_____

Business Organizations

Careers in Business Law

Law, Public Safety, Corrections & Security

SOLAR TURBINES INCORPORATED

Solar Turbines, founded in San Diego, California, in 1927, has evolved into an industry leader in the industrial gas turbine business with over a billion dollars in sales. It incorporates environmental safety and preservation into the designs of its turbines. The company has received a Department of Energy grant for the development of a new generation of high-efficiency, low-emission industrial gas turbines.

The Senior Paralegal/Legal Assistant position at Solar employs business law in many ways by handling certain legal work traditionally done by attorneys. Responsibilities include working on legal records and reviewing and drafting legal documents. The person filling this position is also required to be the network administrator and computer systems and database manager. Good interpersonal skills are required, as well as the ability to work with limited supervision. A four-year degree and ABA paralegal certification or equivalent experience is required.

Think Critically

1. Why is the ability to work with limited supervision important for this position?
2. How valuable are computer skills to this job, and why?

PROJECT | Forms of Business Organization

Project Objectives

- Learn the attributes of the various forms of business organization
- Discover the importance of selecting the appropriate form for a business

BUSINESS HOURS:

MONDAY	TO	
TUESDAY	TO	
WEDNESDAY	TO	
THURSDAY	TO	
FRIDAY	TO	
SATURDAY	TO	
SUNDAY	TO	
HOLIDAYS	TO	

Getting Started

Read the Project Process below. Make a list of any materials you will need.

- Look at all the information you will gather for this project. Decide how you can put this information into an easy-to-understand format.
- List retail, service, manufacturing, and other types of businesses in your area. Be sure to include at least two sole proprietorships, two partnerships, and two corporations.

Project Process

5.1 Call or visit the businesses on your list that are organized as sole proprietorships. What generalizations can you make about their manager/owners, level of investment, professionalism, and future prospects?

5.2 Call or visit the businesses on your list that are organized as partnerships. What generalizations can you make about their manager/owners, level of investment, professionalism, and future prospects?

5.3 Call or visit the businesses on your list that are organized as corporations. What generalizations can you make about their manager/owners, level of investment, professionalism, and future prospects?

Chapter Review

Project Wrap-up   Create a visual presentation of the results of your research. What have you learned? For which of these businesses would you like to work? Why? Which form would you choose for your business? Why?

©Ken Brown, 2009/Used under license from Shutterstock.com

GOALS

Distinguish the fundamental differences in the basic business forms

Explain why someone might choose to become a sole proprietor

KEY TERM

sole proprietorship, p. 122

 JUMP START

Michael Mansfeldian opened his "Robot Factory—Where You Make Your Own Robot" business in April. Six months later a city inspector walked in to see if the business was licensed. The inspector found no license displayed. In fact, Michael had not bothered to obtain one. What will likely happen to Michael and his business as a consequence?

Basic Forms of Business Organization

Although new forms of business organization are constantly being experimented with, they all find their origin in one or a combination of the three basic forms. These are the sole proprietorship, the partnership, and the corporation. These are listed in order of low to high ease and cost of entry, as well as degree of complexity, longevity, intrusiveness of governmental regulation, and the ability to attract professional management.

A **sole proprietorship** is defined as a business owned by one person. It is the simplest and most fundamental of all the forms of business organization. It succeeds or fails based on the owner's abilities, expertise, energy, and interest. In contrast, a corporation requires the personal resources of many and experienced legal advice to operate.

Each one of the basic forms serves a purpose and often reflects the size of the business. A sole proprietorship typically is the smallest in assets, number of employees, sales, and profits. A partnership has a larger size and pool of resources on which to draw. A business in the corporate form is only limited in size and potential resources, human and otherwise, by the level of profits it has earned in the past or may earn in the future.

Realize that as a business grows and perhaps passes through each of these basic forms, its need for professional management and advice increases. For the sole proprietor, a good understanding of the local marketplace and a good business sense might bring success. For a set of partners, having access to areas of expertise, such as from accountants and lawyers, is sometimes necessary, but typically, these types of professionals are not brought into the organization as part of the full-time staff. For large corporations, however, full-time professional managers and advisors are normally considered a necessity.

Why do many professional managers prefer to work for corporations?

Professional managers and advisors have spent many years in school to acquire their professional knowledge and status. From the standpoint of professionals seeking long-term employment and career growth, accepting employment with a sole proprietorship or partnership is risky. A sole proprietorship is dependent on the longevity, knowledge, and the desires of a single person, the sole proprietor alone. Similarly, a partnership legally only lasts until one partner dies or leaves the partnership and, therefore, poses greater risk for a professional seeking long-term, secure employment. As a consequence, a corporation, with its potential for growth and continual existence, normally offers far more long-term opportunities to professional managers and advisors than any other business form.

CheckPOINT

What are the three basic forms of business organization?

_____

_____

The Sole Proprietorship

With a sole proprietorship, a single owner alone is personally liable for the *obligations* of the business. These obligations include providing the business's initial funding (capitalization), making payroll, purchasing supplies, and accepting liability for injuries and property damage caused by employees in the performance of their job duties.

Why be a sole proprietor then? The sole proprietorship is desirable because it is so easy to start. Aside from having a product, a price, and a prospective customer, very little preparation is necessary. The government may enforce such minor requirements as having a tax number or a business license. However, there are few significant consequences for starting without these. "Just do it!"

TEAMWORK

In small groups, brainstorm a list of pros and cons of starting a business as a sole proprietorship. Identify types of businesses that could be organized effectively as sole proprietorships and those that should not be organized using this form.

seems the best way to express both the philosophy and the foresight required to get started as a sole proprietor.

Business Licenses and Tax and Employer Identification Numbers

NETBookmark

Most city, county, and state governments require business owners—including sole proprietors—to obtain business licenses and permits. Access www.cengage.com/school/business/21biz and click on the link for Chapter 5. Read the information from SCORE about business licenses and permits, and then answer: What is the difference between a local business license and a state business license? What is a permit? Name five common permits sole proprietors must often obtain.

www.cengage.com/school/business/21biz

Like other forms of business organization, a sole proprietorship will eventually have to obtain a business license, tax number, and Employer Identification Number. The business license is typically available for a small fee from the local municipal or county government. The tax number is issued by the state. It is used by the business to acquire goods for resale or manufacture without having to pay sales tax on them. This tax number is vital and means a 5 to 10 percent cost savings to the business. Finally, the Employer Identification Number is issued by the federal government. This number generally is used to track liabilities for various taxes and other withholdings.

Advantages and Disadvantages of Sole Proprietorships

Regardless of having to fulfill these minor requirements, the sole proprietorship is far more flexible and responsive to change than the other business forms—if the owner is properly involved in the business. If not, the business is at risk. That's a major weakness of the sole proprietorship as well as its potential strength. Its very existence is the responsibility of one individual, the owner. If the owner loses interest, desire, finances, or physical health, the business typically fails. For this reason, it is difficult to hire long-term professional businesspeople into a sole proprietorship. Both the initial investment in the sole proprietorship and its financial ability to respond to change and opportunity are limited to the resources of the owner. If a sole proprietorship fails, its obligations are enforceable not only against the assets of the business but also against the home, car, furniture, and other possessions of its sole proprietor.

CheckPOINT

Why is a tax number important to a business?

_____

_____

Think Critically

1. What type of background, in terms of education and work experience, do you think the owner of a sole proprietorship should have?

_____

_____

_____

_____

2. Why do you think local governments charge sole proprietors a fee to obtain a business license?

_____

_____

_____

_____

3. What do you think the consequences would be if a sole proprietor failed to obtain an Employer Identification Number from the federal government?

_____

_____

_____

_____

Make Academic Connections

4. **Communication** Contact a sole proprietor in your area. Ask the person about any government requirements the business needs to fulfill. Did the sole proprietor mention additional requirements not discussed in this lesson? If so, what are they? Write a paragraph describing the interview and your findings.

5. **Research** A franchise is another type of business organization that is relatively easy to start. Visit a franchise in your area, or find information about a specific franchise using the Internet. Find out about how to start this franchise. Find out how much money and other resources are necessary to qualify as an owner of the franchise. Write a one-page report on your findings.

6. **Sociology** Make a questionnaire for sole proprietors in your area. Ask about education levels, experience levels, reasons for starting their business, plans for growth of the business, personal plans, personal time, family time, and other indicators of their level of commitment to the enterprise. Consolidate your data and formulate conclusions about sole proprietors.

JUMP START

Winston Blintzki became a limited partner in a partnership organized to build and run a new water park near the beach in Nags Head, North Carolina. He invested $500,000 in it. Soon after the park opened, four people were severely injured when a section of the "mile-high" slide separated from the rest of the slide. As a consequence, the victims slid into thin air and fell 35 feet into a half foot of water. The victims were each awarded damages of more than $5 million. The total amount was far greater than the value of the partnership's assets and insurance coverage. Can Blintzki be held liable for unpaid liability claims against the partnership? Why or why not?

©Nikolay Okhitin, 2009/Used under license from Shutterstock.com

Partnership Basics

The basic partnership form of business is known as the **general partnership**. It is defined as an association of two or more persons to carry on a business for profit as co-owners. The use of the term co-owners implies that each of the partners is individually liable for the obligations of the firm. A partnership involves more legal considerations than does a sole proprietorship.

Uniform Partnership Act

The area of the law relating to general partnerships is governed by the *Uniform Partnership Act (UPA)*. First offered to the states for adoption as law in 1914, the UPA has been enacted by every state except Louisiana. The UPA provides rules for situations that arise from partnerships rather than creating specific steps that must be followed to enter a partnership. The characteristics of the general partnership form include the co-owner's unlimited personal liability for the obligations of the business. So, in addition to being liable for her or his own business mistakes as in a sole proprietorship, a partner also is personally liable for the mistakes of her or his partner(s).

The UPA defines the rights and duties of the partners in relation to the partnership by the following rules.

- Each partner contributes toward the losses sustained by the partnership according to the partner's agreed share in the profits.

- All partners have equal rights in the management and conduct of the business.

- Differences about business operations are decided by a majority of the partners.

These are only a few of the UPA rules that will apply unless a formal partnership agreement specifically states otherwise.

Types of Partners

The flexibility of a partnership is shown by the various types of partners that may use it. For example, *general partners* participate in the management of the partnership, share in the partnership's profits and losses, and are fully liable personally for the partnership's obligations. *Silent partners* are properly and publicly acknowledged as partners but do not participate actively in the management of the partnership. *Secret partners*, on the other hand, are partners but are not known as such publicly. However, they do participate in the management. *Nominal partners* are not actually partners but hold themselves out as such or allow themselves to be held out as such. Finally, *dormant partners* are neither acknowledged publicly as partners nor do they actively participate in the management of the partnership. Typically, these various types of partners are considered fully personally liable for the partnership's obligations.

Limited Partnership

The great potential for liability for a partner in a general partnership has resulted in a statutory alternative being created in most states. This alternative is called the **limited partnership**. Such a partnership is made up of one or more general partners with full personal liability and one or more limited partners whose liability for partnership obligations extends only to the amount of their investment in the business. This is termed *limited liability*. To retain their limited liability, limited partners must not participate in the general management of the business.

The limited partnership form of business was authorized by the Revised Uniform Limited Partnership Act (RULPA) in 1916. Changes were made in the versions of RULPA created in 1976 and 2001. Almost all states have enacted one of the RULPA versions or another. Note that because it is in statutory form, the formation procedure for a limited partnership must be strictly followed.

COMMUNICATE

With another student, think of a business that you'd like to operate together as a partnership. Make up a partnership agreement for this business. Put the agreement in writing.

This is not true for the formation of a general partnership. If the procedure for a limited partnership is not properly followed, the would-be limited partners will be held fully personally liable as general partners.

Creation of a General Partnership

There are two principal ways of forming a general partnership. The first way is by express agreement of the persons involved. The second way a partnership is formed results from a court determination that a partnership exists because of how certain parties do business with one another.

By Agreement Partnerships are most often created by express agreement of the parties. The *partnership agreement* is a detailed statement of the terms and conditions for running the business to which the partners agree. The agreement can be oral or in writing. The agreement cannot be oral, however, if the partnership is involved in the acquisition and sale of real estate or if it conflicts with the statute of frauds requirement for a writing.

By Court Acknowledgment A court may determine that a partnership exists because of how certain parties do business with one another. If a person maintains in court that a partnership exists, the court will examine the business dealings of the alleged partners for existing evidence

What is the purpose of a partnership agreement?

of the partnership. The most common evidence is the sharing of profits. If the court discovers that profits are shared, it will hold that a partnership exists unless satisfactory evidence to the contrary is presented.

Once satisfactory evidence has been presented, the court will presume there is a partnership. However, the opposing side may still introduce evidence to show that the court's presumption is wrong. The court will not look for evidence on its own. If evidence of a partnership is found, it is then up to the party denying that a partnership exists to disprove the court's findings.

CheckPOINT

What are the two ways in which partnerships are formed?

_____

_____

Operation of a Partnership

The rules determining the operation of a partnership may be spelled out in a partnership agreement. If an express agreement does not exist or is incomplete, some or all of the rules of operation are governed by the Uniform Partnership Act. The following discussion reflects the UPA rules.

Management of Partnerships

Under the UPA, any of the partners can conduct the day-to-day operations of the business. Each partner has equal rights in the management of the ordinary course of business no matter how small that partner's percentage of ownership may be. Any difference of opinion among the partners over routine matters is to be resolved by a majority vote of the partners. If that method fails, then any previous pattern of conducting business is followed, if appropriate. If no previous pattern exists or if the failure to resolve the issue harms the business, the partnership must be dissolved.

Certain managerial decisions require agreement by all the partners. For example, using partnership property as collateral, bringing in a new partner, and selling the partnership's real property require the consent of all the partners. Also, under the UPA, partners can assign their partnership interests, such as profits, to nonpartners. If this is done, those who receive such interests do not also receive the right to take part in the management of the partnership business.

Profits, Losses, and Property Rights

Each partner is entitled to an equal share in the profits and losses of the partnership unless agreement to the contrary has been reached. However, it is often to the tax advantage of partners who have extensive income from outside of the partnership to take a larger share of the partnership's losses than is taken by those who do not have other income. Such an allocation can easily be provided for in the partnership agreement. Under the UPA, partners may call for an accounting of the partnership business to determine profits, losses, and other matters whenever this is "just and reasonable."

The UPA also gives each partner a co-ownership in partnership property. This *tenancy in partnership* provides that each partner has an equal right to possess specific partnership property for partnership purposes. This right, unlike the partner's interest in the profits of the partnership, cannot be assigned to another party. Likewise, specific partnership property cannot be used for personal purposes by any partner without the consent of the other partners. Consequently, a partner's creditors cannot assert their rights against specific partnership property, whether or not the property is in that partner's possession. If a partner dies, the deceased partner's rights in specific partnership property pass to the surviving partners. The surviving spouse, heirs, or next of kin cannot claim specific partnership property.

Liability for Business Operations

All of the provisions of the tenancy in partnership act to provide the best possible opportunity for preserving the partnership's business in the face of individual misfortune. However, the partnership is liable for torts that a partner or an employee commits while engaged in the partnership's business. Each partner can be sued, or perhaps released from liability, separately without affecting the case against the other partners. Also, all or several of the partners can be sued at once. If sued separately and recovered against in full, a partner is entitled to seek contributions from the other partners. If necessary, a partner may secure such contributions by court action.

If a partner commits a crime to further the partnership's interests, that partner is separately liable for the offense. A contract action brought against the partnership must be brought against the partners jointly. The judgment received or the release granted applies to all of the partners.

Is a general partner liable for the actions of another partner? Explain.

©Mark Stout Photography, 2009/Used under license from Shutterstock.com

Fiduciary Duty above All

Each partner owes a **fiduciary duty** in conducting the partnership's business, which means that the partner must act in good faith and put the partnership's interest above her or his own. Using partnership funds or other property for personal gain violates this duty, as does competing against the partnership. The courts will hold the partner accountable to the partnership for any individual gain that he or she receives while on partnership business.

How Are Partnerships Ended?

A partnership's existence may have to be brought to a legal end because of intentional actions of the partners, because of the automatic operation of the law, or because a court has declared that the partnership should end. Any one of these possibilities may result in a *dissolution of the partnership*. The UPA defines a dissolution as a change whereby any partner ceases to be associated with carrying on the partnership's business.

TEAMWORK

In small groups, discuss the importance of fiduciary duty in a partnership. What happens to the partnership when one of the partners disregards this duty?

The dissolution of a partnership does not necessarily mean that the partnership's business must end. Often the partnership agreement provides a way for the remaining partners to buy out the interest of the departing partner. If not, the partnership business will have to be concluded and terminated.

By the Intentional Acts of a Partner Many partnership agreements set the time period that the partnership will remain in existence. Once that term has run or a specified event has occurred, such as gross earnings falling below a certain amount, the partnership is dissolved. Some partnership agreements tie dissolution to the accomplishment of a partnership's purpose, such as the construction of a bridge. If nothing is set in the partnership agreement on the term of the partnership, then the partnership is considered to be "at will." Any partner can dissolve a partnership at will at any time without incurring liability for doing so.

By Action of Law Certain events dissolve partnerships automatically. These events are identified in various laws. For example, the law states that the death of a partner ends the partnership. The bankruptcy of a partner or the bankruptcy of the partnership has the same result. The loss of professional status or license also could bring on the dissolution.

By Court Judgment Some circumstances may cause the partnership to be inoperable but do not bring on its automatic dissolution under the law or the partnership agreement. In these cases, a court can be petitioned with the facts of the matter. The court will judge whether or not the partnership can or should be continued. Typical reasons for such petitions are

- Disputes among the partners that cannot be reconciled
- A significant willful breach of the partnership agreement
- The inability to carry on the partnership's business except at a loss
- The incapacity of a partner to carry out the partnership agreement

Because dissolution of a partnership affects the third parties that deal with it, the law has special provisions relating to the notice of dissolution owed to third parties. Creditors must receive direct personal notice of the dissolution. Others, until they receive implied or express notice of the dissolution, are protected if they continue to deal with the partnership in the same manner in which they had dealt with it previously.

Winding Up

What is involved in winding up a partnership?

Winding up a partnership can be accomplished either according to a procedure set in the partnership agreement or according to UPA rules. It requires concluding all business and selling the partnership property. After the cash accumulated in this way has been used to satisfy the partnership's debts, any remaining funds are distributed to the partners according to the percentage of the profits each normally receives. The partnership then ceases to function, and the partnership agreement is terminated.

It is important to remember three things about this procedure. First, until the partnership has been fully wound up, the partners still owe a fiduciary duty to one another. Second, once the procedure has begun, the partners must act only in ways that contribute to the winding-up process. Third, in paying off the partnership's creditors, nonpartner creditors receive their payment before partner-creditors receive theirs.

Obviously, destroying an ongoing profitable business seldom does anyone any good in the long term. The employees lose their livelihood. The economy loses a viable participant. Even the partners who receive a payout from the process probably would get a better return on their money if the business continued to operate. Nonetheless, if the business has to be wound up, following a fair and orderly procedure in the winding-up stages is the best insurance against subsequent lawsuits.

CheckPOINT

What are three ways in which dissolution of a partnership can be initiated?

_____

_____

Think Critically

1. For a business owner, what makes a partnership more potentially dangerous from a liability standpoint than a sole proprietorship?

2. How does the constitutional guarantee of the freedom to contract impact the UPA and RULPA?

3. Do you think an attorney should be consulted in the formation of a partnership agreement? What factors argue for consulting an attorney? What factors argue against it?

4. What is a partner's fiduciary duty to the partnership?

5. You just graduated from an MBA program with a hot idea for a business, but you need capital. What form of partnership, general or limited, would you consider? Why?

Make Academic Connections

6. **Ecology** How could the limited partnership form of business be used to avoid liability for improper handling of hazardous waste? What could be done to prevent such a misuse of this business form? Give a presentation of your findings in class.

7. **Marketing** Read the financial section of your newspaper. Note the details in the ads that are seeking investments in various projects. Are any of them looking for general partners? Limited partners? What conclusions can you draw from this? Choose one ad, and write a one-page report that describes the investments and answers these questions.

JUMP START

Several French teachers from a city's public school system plan to form a business that will conduct tours of France for their students and others during the summer. The teachers plan to be the owners, directors, officers, managers, employees, and shareholders. They need to choose a form of organization. One teacher is concerned about personal liability should one of the students be injured during a tour. Another wants to avoid the double taxation that would result from the corporate form of business. What legal form of organization should they choose to avoid both of these issues?

Corporation Basics

The corporation offers the best limited liability protection for investors. It is the form of business that almost all large firms choose. A **corporation** is defined as a legal entity or artificial person created through the authority of federal or state law. It can be owned by one or more persons, other corporations, a governmental body, or a combination of all of these. It can sue or be sued without its investors being exposed to the risk of losing personal assets to pay any corporate debts that result. Also, it continues in existence beyond the withdrawal or death of its owners due to the free transferability of ownership in the form of certificates of ownership called **shares of stock**.

The protection of limited liability and the possibility of perpetual existence make the corporation the most popular form for attracting capital investment. Of course, the large size of some corporations makes them unresponsive to the best interests of some of their owners and, all too often, to the immediate challenges of the marketplace. Also, the enormous earnings of some corporations and the power that comes with those earnings have made corporations the target of public criticism and, perhaps more important, of almost every government body with taxing authority. Even so, if dollars were votes, the corporate form would be elected the world's most popular form of business ownership for investors.

Although corporations are far outnumbered by sole proprietorships and partnerships, corporations do most of the business in this country. This is because the corporation has features that are essential for large-scale enterprises. Some of these features are attractive to small businesses too.

Why is the corporation the form of business chosen most often by businesses with large amounts of assets?

Advantages of Corporations

The advantages of corporations include perpetual life, limited liability, transferability of ownership interests, and the ability to attract large sums of capital and professional management.

Perpetual Life Unlike the sole proprietorship, a corporation is a legal entity separate and distinct from its owners and managers. Therefore, it can continue to function after they die. Under the law, a corporation may continue indefinitely with new owners, managers, and employees.

Limited Liability The corporation itself is liable without limit for its debts, but its creditors normally cannot collect claims against the corporation from people who own shares in it. Individual stockholders stand to lose only the amount they have already invested in the business. This limited liability makes the corporate form of business organization desirable for investors.

Under unusual conditions, courts may hold the shareholders personally responsible for corporate debts. This practice is called "piercing the corporate veil." A court may take this extreme action, more likely with small corporations, if shareholders fail to keep corporate assets separate from their own or if they hide behind the corporate form for improper purposes, such as to avoid debts that they should pay personally.

Transferability of Ownership Interests A major advantage of the corporate form over the partnership form is the ease of transferring ownership interests in the firm. Normally, individual owners can sell their interests in the corporation without the consent of other owners and without disturbing the

DID YOU KNOW ?

More than half of the major corporations in the United States that make up the Fortune 500 list of leading American companies are incorporated in Delaware. This is due to that state's supportive laws, pro-business attitude, and separate court system for handling legal issues related to Delaware corporations.

Tech Literacy

TWITTERING THE STOCK MARKET

For over a decade, the Internet has had a major impact on investing in corporations due to inexpensive online trading services and the ability to do personal research. Even so, many investors continued to use brokerage services due to the informational networks and analytical abilities of the stockbrokers. However, the popularity of paying for professional brokerage services has been diminished of late by the real-time immediacy and incisive, diverse information provided on various Twitter locations, such as StockTwits.

THINK CRITICALLY

Compared to working with traditional stockbrokers, what do you think are the disadvantages, if any, of using Twitter locations for trading information?

TEAMWORK

Divide into investment firms of three or more individuals each. Your firm is to invest a hypothetical $10,000 in American stocks of your choosing. You may buy and sell the stocks at will for the next month but must pay a 3 percent commission on the dollar amount of each trade. Keep profit and loss records of each transaction and present a summary report of your investment firm's results at the end of each week. At the end of the month, report on your experiences and what you have learned.

company's operations. The stock of most large corporations is bought and sold, or traded, on the major stock exchanges. By contacting a stockbroker, any person may buy or sell shares of any listed stock within minutes when the stock exchanges are open.

Large Sums of Capital Investors feel reasonably secure when buying stock in corporations. Their liability as owners is limited to the amount they have invested, and they may readily sell their shares or buy more. Further, the corporation may have perpetual life, outlasting present owners, directors, and employees, all of whom may be replaced without terminating the business. As a result, large sums of money may be raised by the sale of corporate stock. Small and large investments by thousands of persons and institutions are combined to fund giant corporations.

Professional Management Because they can and do raise substantial amounts of capital, efficient corporations generally have greater financial strength than do other forms of business organization. This enables corporations to attract talented employees by offering generous salaries and fringe benefits. Also, because the corporation is not automatically dissolved by the death of any owner or manager, it usually provides better assurance of long-term employment.

Disadvantages of the Corporate Form

There are some important disadvantages to the corporate form. Unlike the earnings of a sole proprietorship or partnership, the earnings of a corporation are subject to *double taxation*. Because the corporation is considered a separate artificial person, it is taxed on its earnings. Then, when earnings are paid out to the owners (stockholders) as *dividends*, the earnings are taxed a second time, since the dividends must be reported as income on the stockholders' personal tax returns.

The Bay Minette Flower Shop had flourished for years as a partnership. Finally, the partnership incorporated the business. Both while a partnership and after incorporating, the business had been supplied by a wholesaler, M & M Florist, Inc. Although they continued their business relationship for many years afterwards, M & M was never told of Bay Minette's incorporation. Finally, however, after a business downturn, M & M sued Bay Minette and its owners for an overdue debt. As a consequence of the incorporation, the owners of Bay Minette refused to pay the corporate debt from their personal assets.

THINK CRITICALLY
Should the court "pierce the corporate veil" and require the owners to pay the debt from their personal fortunes if the corporate assets are inadequate to do so? Why or why not?

In addition to the taxation disadvantage, it is costlier and more troublesome to organize a corporation than it is to organize a sole proprietorship or partnership. Further, large corporations are subject to extensive regulation of the sale of their stocks and bonds to the public. Finally, juries sometimes tend to favor individuals in legal disputes with corporations. But, overall, the advantages of the corporation usually outweigh its disadvantages, especially for big enterprises.

Types of Corporations

Corporations are classified according to their place of incorporation and purpose. If a corporation is chartered in a particular state, it is a *domestic corporation* in that state. A corporation doing business in one state but chartered in another is termed a *foreign corporation*. Finally, a corporation doing business in a state but that is chartered in another nation is an *alien corporation* in that state.

In terms of purpose, a corporation is either public or private. A *public corporation* is established for a governmental purpose. Incorporated cities, state hospitals, and state universities are public corporations. Private citizens establish *private corporations* for business or charitable purposes.

Sometimes a corporation owned by private citizens is called a "public corporation" on the stock markets because members of the general public can own its stock. This designation is not a legal one but does differentiate it from a private corporation, where only one or a small number of shareholders own the stock. The latter type is also known as a *close* or *closely held corporation*.

Private corporations are further classified as profit making, nonprofit, and public service corporations. A *profit-making corporation* is a private corporation organized to produce a financial profit for its owners. Examples include banks, manufacturing and merchandising companies, and airlines.

A *nonprofit corporation* is organized for a social, charitable, or educational purpose. It may have revenues that exceed expenses, but it does not distribute any of these earnings to its owners as profits. If a nonprofit corporation engages in business for profit, it must, like any other business, pay income taxes. Churches, colleges, fraternal societies, and like organizations are typically organized as nonprofit corporations.

Finally, a *public service corporation*, also called a *public utility*, generally is a private company that furnishes an essential public service. Electric, gas, and water companies are examples. However, they are closely regulated as to the quality of service they must provide, the prices they can charge, and the profit margin they may earn. Competition in providing such services, which are needed by most persons, would be needlessly wasteful.

Check**POINT**

List three advantages of the corporate form of business.

_____

_____

_____

Creation, Ownership, Management, and Powers of Corporations

To create a corporation, an application for incorporation must be filed with a state official in the state in which incorporation is sought. This application contains the *articles of incorporation*, which serve as the corporation's basic plan of operation. The articles are signed and submitted by one or more persons called *incorporators*. At least one of the incorporators must have legal capacity to enter into a binding contract. Thus, the incorporators cannot all be minors. However, another corporation may be an incorporator.

To indicate approval, a state may issue a certificate of incorporation or a *charter*. Once the corporation receives the corporate charter, units of ownership called shares of stock are sold. The owners, or shareholders (also referred to as stockholders), meet and elect a board of individuals to administer the corporation. This group is called *the board of directors*. The board of directors hires the corporate officers and managers who will run the company on a day-to-day basis. These officers and managers use the money received from the initial sale of stock to start doing business. They buy equipment, supplies, and inventory. They hire workers. As goods and services are produced and sold, money flows into the business. If the business is profitable, earnings are either paid out to the shareholders as dividends and/or reinvested in the business. Later, to assist in expansion, more shares of stock may be sold and/or money may be borrowed.

Types of Stock

Stock may have a *par value*, which is the face value printed on the certificate. If it does not have a par value, it is termed "no par stock" and is sold at a price set by the board of directors of the corporation. When either par or no-par stock changes hands in later transfers, the price may be higher or lower. This *market price* is determined by many factors, including past and expected future profits of the business.

What is the most important difference between common stock and preferred stock?

Corporations may have one or more kinds of stock. *Common stock* is the basic type and conveys the right to vote in corporate elections. Shareholders of common stock typically have one vote per share owned. They may receive dividends. *Dividends* are distributions of profits earned by the corporation. To attract additional funds from investors who want greater assurance of payment of dividends, some corporations issue *preferred stock*. Owners of preferred stock usually have no voting power but are legally entitled to a stated dividend, if there are enough earnings in the current accounting period to pay it, before the common shareholders receive anything. For example, the preferred shareholder may be entitled to receive $7 per share each year before any distribution of dividends is made to the common shareholders. The common shareholders then share in the remaining earnings *pro rata*, or in proportion to the number of shares owned. If profits are high, the common shareholders may ultimately get more money than the preferred shareholders. As a consequence, another form of stock was developed called *participating preferred stock*. The holder of this type of stock is paid the stated dividend, say $7, and then the preferred shareholder shares in the remaining distributed earnings pro rata along with the common shareholders. Preferred shareholders generally have a priority right to be repaid the face value of their stock from the corporation's funds in the event of liquidation. *Liquidation* occurs when all of the business assets are sold, all debts are paid, and the corporation's existence is ended.

Corporate Management

A corporation is a legal person in the eyes of the law. However, it must act through human agents. No shareholder, not even one that owns most or all the stock, can act for the corporation or bind it by contract merely because of such ownership. Regardless, shareholders indirectly control the affairs of a corporation by electing the board of directors. They also have the power to vote on major issues, such as changing the corporate articles, merging with another company, or selling out in a corporate takeover.

The directors are responsible for the overall management of the corporation. They are *fiduciaries*, which makes them duty-bound to act in good faith and with due care to oversee the corporation and create its general policies. They must not act fraudulently or illegally. Most states apply the standard of the *Model Business Corporation Act*. This requires that the directors act "in a manner reasonably believed to be in the best interests of the corporation and with such care as an ordinary prudent person in a like position would use under similar circumstances." Failure to do so can make the director liable for damages to the shareholders.

The number of directors varies among corporations. Most states allow the shareholders to determine the number. Some states require at least three. Other states require only one director, who also can be the sole officer and sole shareholder. This gives the corporation the attributes of a sole proprietorship plus the advantage of limited liability for its owner.

The directors set major goals and determine basic policies, such as whether to sell for cash, credit, or both, and whether to expand or reduce operations in a given area. They appoint and set the salaries of the top officers of the company, typically the president, vice president, secretary, and treasurer. Acting together, the directors have the power to make contracts for the corporation. However, they delegate the day-to-day duties of running the business to the officers they have selected.

Officers are legally accountable to the corporation for willful or negligent acts that cause loss to it. However, neither shareholders, directors, nor other officers can be held personally liable to parties outside the corporation for honest errors of judgment made in exercising their corporate powers. This is referred to as the **business judgment rule**.

Corporate Powers

The officers and other legal agents of the corporation may use any legal means to conduct authorized business. The corporation has the power to

- Make contracts
- Borrow money and incur other liabilities
- Lend money and acquire assets, including all forms of real and personal property
- Make, indorse, and accept commercial paper, or orders or promises to pay money
- Issue various types of stock and bonds (*Bonds* are long-term notes issued in return for money borrowed from a lender or lenders. They are usually secured by a mortgage or deposit of collateral with the lender. Unsecured bonds, called *debentures*, can also be issued.)
- Mortgage, pledge, lease, sell, or assign property

- Buy back its own stock, unless this would make it impossible for the corporation to pay its debts or to pay off any superior class of stock

- Acquire and hold stock in other corporations provided the result would not violate antitrust laws

- Make reasonable donations or gifts for civic or charitable purposes to promote goodwill in accord with corporate social responsibility

- Hire and fire agents, independent contractors, and ordinary employees

- Establish pension, profit sharing, and other incentive plans for employees

- Sue and be sued

- Utilize other implied powers

Why would a corporation support a charitable cause?

A corporation may do any legal act that is necessary or convenient for the execution of its express powers. This would extend to such matters as doing pure and applied research and development (R&D) work; leasing space and equipment; advertising; and buying life, health, and liability insurance for officers and other employees.

Termination of Corporations

A variety of causes may bring about the dissolution or termination of a corporation. The cause may be by specification of the incorporators or agreement of the shareholders, by the corporation losing its charter, by consolidation or merger, by bankruptcy, or by court order.

Incorporator Specification or Shareholder Agreement A corporation terminates upon expiration of the agreed-upon period of its existence as stipulated in its articles of incorporation. A corporation may also end before the agreed-upon time if the shareholders voluntarily vote to end it.

Loss of Charter A corporation that has been guilty of certain acts may face state-initiated court proceedings, resulting in the loss of its charter. Examples of such acts are

1. Fraudulent submission of articles of incorporation

2. Flagrant misuse of corporate powers

3. Repeated violation of the law

Loss of a charter is rare because the state does not monitor corporate affairs, and persons who have a grievance can seek private relief in court.

Consolidation or Merger A consolidation of corporations can occur with the approval of the boards of directors and a set majority of the shareholders in each of the corporations involved. In a *consolidation,* the two corporations cease to exist and a new corporation is formed. In a *merger*, one corporation is absorbed by another. The surviving corporation retains its charter and identity, and the other disappears. Again, approval must be given by the directors and by the shareholders of the merging corporations.

A combination through either consolidation or merger must not violate antitrust laws by interfering unreasonably with free competition. An illegal monopoly occurs when one company acquires the power to control the supply of goods, exclude competitors, and set prices. It is also illegal for two or more companies to set prices jointly or to allocate marketing areas because this reduces free competition. U.S. antitrust laws have been amended to permit competing companies to form partnerships for joint research in order to meet global competition. Thus, for example, it is legal for two or more American car companies to do joint research on materials, oil, reformulated fuel, batteries, and electronic systems for vehicles.

Bankruptcy Bankruptcy does not in itself cause dissolution. However, some bankruptcy proceedings leave the corporation without assets with which to do business. In addition, some state statutes provide that when a corporation is unable to pay its debts, its creditors may force dissolution upon it.

Court Order Occasionally, a corporation's assets are seriously threatened with irreparable harm because the board of directors or the shareholders cannot resolve a dispute. In some states, this situation would permit a court to order dissolution if interested parties petition for it. This rarely happens, however.

CheckPOINT

What are five ways in which corporations may be terminated?

_____

_____

Alternatives to the Full Corporate Form

Over the years, the basic corporate form has been modified to accommodate a variety of needs. Although the "C" corporate form (named for and governed by subchapter C of the Internal Revenue Code) remains the choice for large corporations, other forms are available, typically for small businesses. These include the S corporation, the limited liability corporation (LLC), and the limited liability partnership (LLP).

S Corporations

A small corporation that elects to be treated as an S corporation can avoid double taxation of earnings. S corporations are organized under subchapter S of the Internal Revenue Code. The earnings are treated the same as a gain (or loss) from a partnership and only taxed at the individual owner's level. The S corporation is not so much a corporate form as it is a tax status. To acquire this status, a business must first form itself as a corporation in the normal fashion and then make a qualified filing with the IRS. In order to qualify as an S corporation under the IRS code, the business must satisfy several requirements.

What are the requirements for an S corporation?

- **Timely Filing**   A corporation wanting to be taxed as an S corporation must file the appropriate form with the IRS before March 15 of the tax year in which the election is to be effective. The election must reflect the unanimous choice of the shareholders. Any election to resume being taxed as a C corporation must also be the unanimous decision of shareholders.

- **Domestic Corporation**   The S corporation status is reserved for businesses incorporated in the United States.

- **Identity of Shareholders**   Only natural persons, estates, or certain types of trusts can be shareholders in an S corporation. Other corporations, partnerships, nonqualifying trusts, and non-resident aliens cannot.

- **Number of Shareholders**   The corporation must have 100 or fewer shareholders.

- **Classes of Stock**   The corporation can have only one class of stock. However, the shareholders in that class are not required to have the same voting rights.

Limited Liability Corporations

For years, the best forms of business organization for small businesses were the limited partnership and the subchapter S corporation. These forms had flaws and limitations. Consequently, in 1977 legislators in Wyoming took a bold step toward providing business organization alternatives by passing a statute that authorized creation of a limited liability corporation. They based their actions on forms of business organizations that existed in Europe and South America. In essence, the limited liability corporation (LLC) offers limited liability protection and taxation as a partnership, but lacks the limitations of the subchapter S or limited partnership alternatives.

For more than a decade, the LLC itself remained an alternative only in Wyoming and Florida. Interest in LLCs grew in 1988, when the Internal Revenue Service ruled that LLCs would be taxed as partnerships at the federal level. By late 1997, every state had an LLC-empowering statute.

Formation of a Limited Liability Corporation (LLC)   Similar to a corporation or limited partnership, a limited liability corporation must be formed and operated in accordance with the law in the state in which it is organized. In most states, an LLC is formed by filing *articles of organization* in an appropriate state office, usually the Secretary of State's office.

The owners of an LLC are known as *members*. As with C corporations, their liability is limited to the amount that they have invested in the business. The earnings of the LLC, however, are taxed as a partnership. This eliminates the double taxation that occurs with the C corporation. However, some states allow certain members to declare themselves as fully personally liable at the time of organization. This is often a plus with potential creditors.

The significant advantages that make LLCs more attractive than other forms of organization are as follows.

1. There are no limitations on the number of members.

2. There are no limitations as to whom or what can be a stockholder in an LLC. Therefore, foreign nationals, corporations, and other business entities can all be shareholders.

3. Members are allowed to participate completely in managing the business. There are no worries of losing the limited liability status for members who do manage, as might be the case even under RULPA.

Tax problems associated with transferring assets from a partnership or corporation to the LLC are the only significant disadvantage of LLCs.

Limited Liability Partnerships

With all the advantages of the LLC, it is hard to imagine a need for any other small business form. However, some already-existing business entities have found it difficult to convert to an LLC. This is especially the case for partnerships constructed for professionals, such as doctors and lawyers. The difficulty is not limited to taxation problems but extends to the complexity of ending the partnership, valuing the interests, and then reestablishing the business entity as an LLC. In response to these problems, Texas created the limited liability partnership in 1991. The **limited liability partnership (LLP)** offers ease of conversion from an existing partnership, avoidance of double taxation, and partial limited liability protection. Within six years, almost all states had enacted LLP statutes.

Under the majority of the LLP statutes, the limited liability protection shields against the consequences of the tortious acts of others involved in the partnership. The Texas statute, for example, protects innocent partners from the consequences of errors, omissions, negligence, incompetence, or malfeasance stemming from partnership operations. Therefore, if a partner commits professional malpractice and the recovery from it exceeds the amount of liability insurance coverage the partnership or that individual carries, the other partners will not have their personal fortunes endangered.

CheckPOINT

What are three limited liability alternatives to the full corporate form?

_____

_____

Think Critically

1. Why can a corporation continue to exist beyond the life of its owners?

_____

_____

2. What do you think is the most valuable attribute of a corporation? Why?

_____

_____

3. Why does the government closely regulate public service corporations?

_____

_____

4. What is the business judgment rule?

_____

_____

5. What do governments get in return for allowing the S corporation, LLC, and LLP forms of business organization to exist?

_____

_____

6. What do you think might have brought about the birth of the LLP?

_____

_____

Make Academic Connections

7. **Careers** Using a job search web site, find information on specific management-level jobs that interest you in both large and small corporations. Compare the salaries and benefits offered. Do the jobs at the large or small companies appeal to you more? Explain your answer.

8. **Arts** Public radio and television stations in many cities are organized as nonprofit corporations. These stations often raise operating revenue through on-air appeals to their listening and viewing audiences. Write a paragraph supporting or opposing the need for "public" stations in today's media.

9. **Business Math** Find out the state and federal tax rates on corporations in your state. Consider businesses with profits of $100,000, $1,000,000, and $100,000,000. Calculate how much the LLC or S corporations would save for each of these businesses over the full corporate form. Given this savings, why would corporations choose the full corporate form?

Chapter Summary

5.1 **Sole Proprietorships**

A. The basic forms of business organization are the sole proprietorship, the partnership, and the corporation.

B. The sole proprietorship is popular because of its simplicity, but it needs to obtain a business license, state tax number, and federal Employee Identification Number.

5.2 **Partnerships**

A. Partnerships are more complex to form than sole proprietorships. A good partnership agreement is important.

B. In general partnerships, each partner has full personal liability. In limited partnerships, only one partner need be fully personally liable.

5.3 **Corporations**

A. Corporations are legal entities, separate from owners, and have perpetual life, limited liability, easy transfer of ownership, and the ability to attract large sums of capital and professional management. They are complex to organize and subject to extensive regulation.

B. Corporations are formed under state law and managed by a board of directors that delegates day-to-day operations to officers it selects.

C. Corporation types include public, private, closely held, profit-making, nonprofit, and public service corporations. Alternatives to the full corporate form include S corporations, LLCs, and LLPs.

Vocabulary Builder

Choose the term that best fits the definition. Write the letter of the answer in the space provided. Some terms may not be used.

_____ 1. An association of two or more persons to carry on a business for profit as co-owners

_____ 2. A business owned by one person

_____ 3. A legal entity created through the authority of federal or state law

_____ 4. Units of ownership in a corporation

_____ 5. Partnership form authorized by state statute requiring at least one general partner but allowing limited partners

_____ 6. A responsibility to act in good faith and to put the organization's best interest ahead of your own

_____ 7. Form of business organization offering limited liability protection, taxation as a partnership, and few of the restrictions of the S corporation or limited partnership alternatives

_____ 8. A business form easily converted from a general or limited partnership that avoids double taxation and offers limited liability protection

_____ 9. The owners of a corporation

a. business judgment rule

b. corporation

c. fiduciary duty

d. general partnership

e. limited liability corporation (LLC)

f. limited liability partnership (LLP)

g. limited partnership

h. S corporation

i. shareholders

j. shares of stock

k. sole proprietorship

Review Concepts

Point Your Browser
www.cengage.com/
school/business/21biz

10. Which business forms offer limited liability to some or all of their owners? Why is it important to an investor/owner?

_____

_____

_____

11. What is the significance of being the general partner in a limited partnership?

_____

_____

_____

12. Why should a professional manager carefully consider going to work for a sole proprietorship?

_____

_____

_____

13. Why and how did limited liability partnerships come about?

_____

_____

_____

14. What form of business organization is subject to double taxation?

_____

_____

_____

_____

15. What are the requirements of an S corporation?

_____

_____

_____

16. Where did the concept of the LLC begin?

_____

_____

_____

17. For what types of debts are the partners in an LLP personally liable?

_____

_____

_____

18. Are any of the members of an LLC personally liable for the corporate debts? If so, which members are personally liable?

_____

_____

_____

19. Which one of the various limited liability forms of business organization do you consider to be most likely to survive a depression? Why?

_____

_____

_____

Apply What You Learned

20. Why are most of the major U.S. corporations not LLCs or other alternative business forms?

_____

_____

_____

21. If a state government discovers it is losing too much tax revenue by not taxing LLCs and S corporations, what would you recommend that it do? Can a state act alone in such a matter? Why or why not?

_____

_____

_____

_____

22. Should corporate managers be able to avoid criminal and civil prosecutions for the mistakes they make by hiding behind the business judgment rule? Why or why not?

_____

_____

_____

23. What role do corporations play in electing government leaders? What role do they play in enacting legislation? Are the roles played by corporations in elections and passing legislation a good idea? Why or why not?

_____

_____

_____

_____

_____

Make Academic Connections

24. **Environment** What corporations that you know of work to protect the environment? What sort of interest (profit-motive, societal, ethical, philosophical) do these corporations have in doing so? Justify your answer(s) in a class presentation.

25. **Sports Law** Several decades ago, a classic antitrust case involving alleged restraint of trade developed around a truly amazing athlete. After leading the United States to a gold medal in the Mexico City Olympics at the age of 19 and leading the NCAA by averaging 32 points and 21.5 rebounds in his sophomore year at the University of Detroit, Spencer Haywood left the college ranks and, citing the hardship of his family, signed with the Denver Rockets of the ABA. After his first season with the pro team, he was named both Rookie of the Year and the league's Most Valuable Player. The ABA was disintegrating, so he sought to jump to the Seattle Supersonics of the NBA. Unfortunately, he was blocked by the then-current NBA rule that disallowed signing a player until that player's high school class could have graduated college. This "four-year rule" was, alleged Haywood in his case filing, a restraint on trade and thereby illegal as a violation of the Sherman Antitrust Act. In your judgment, is the rule illegal, and if so, should it be overturned by the court? Why or why not?

_____

_____

_____

26. **Marketing** Look at the *Yellow Pages* section on attorneys. Correlate the biggest ads with the legal specialties. Where do business-oriented attorneys rate in the correlation? Write a paragraph on your findings.

27. **Business Law** For a business, how important do you think it is to choose the proper legal form of business from the start?

_____

_____

Ethical Dilemma

28. Consider the Haywood case in Problem 25 above. Was the "four-year rule" ethically justifiable from the standpoint of the NBA? From the standpoint of the players, both in the NBA and in college? Why or why not?

_____

_____

_____

_____

CHAPTER 6

Law and Finance

Careers in Business Law

JPMORGAN CHASE

JPMorgan Chase & Co. is the third largest commercial bank in the United States. The company serves millions of customers and offers a wide range of banking services. Additional services include investments, credit cards, insurance, financial planning, mutual funds, and annuities.

Collectors for JPMorgan Chase work directly with customers who have failed to repay their consumer loans as scheduled. They review and analyze customer financial data to evaluate the debtor's capacity to pay. They also work with the customers to reach a mutually agreeable strategy for payment of the loan. They determine whether legal action will be necessary to collect the loan.

JPMorgan Chase Collectors need four or more years of collection experience, with a specific area of specialization, such as home equity or auto finance defaults. Strong negotiation skills also are necessary.

Think Critically

1. What personality characteristics would a Collector need to possess? Why?
2. Why do you think a Collector would need to have strong negotiation skills? What other skills do you think would be helpful?

Project Objectives

- Recognize the impact of legal requirements in the area of personal and business finance.
- Know and be able to apply the law to checks, drafts, promissory notes, secured instruments, and other debtor/creditor relationships.

> **PROMISSORY NOTE**
>
> $4,000   Atlantic City, New Jersey   March 17, 20—
>
> 60 days from sight I, Eric Camley, promise to pay to the order of First National Bank four thousand and no/100 dollars.
>
> Payable at the First National Bank, 461 Boardwalk, Atlantic City, New Jersey with interest at 10% a year.
>
> *Eric Camley*
> Eric Camley

Getting Started

Read through the Project Process below. Make a list of information sources needed to complete the requirements of the project.

Project Process

6.1 List the various types of commercial paper. Identify where you and others close to you encounter each type. List these points of contact. Obtain samples of the paper used and display them in class.

6.2 Examine various advertisements in newspapers, in magazines, in direct mailings, on television, online, and so forth. List the various types of sale and lease offers that are accompanied by financing programs. List the terms of these programs, and compare the secured with the unsecured programs. What are your observations?

6.3 Look in the *Yellow Pages* for bankruptcy attorneys in your area. Prepare a list of questions as a prospective client. For example: How much will it cost? What are your fees? How will bankruptcy affect my credit standing? Will I be able to keep my home and car? How much will my creditors receive? Have your previous clients been able to reestablish themselves? If so, how long did it take and under what conditions? Call the attorneys, interview the willing ones, and compare their answers. What are your observations?

Chapter Review

Project Wrap-up Publish a booklet of advice on the use of commercial paper, secured transactions, and bankruptcy.

GOALS

List the various types of commercial paper and describe the use and proper negotiation of each type

Explain electronic funds transfers (EFTs)

KEY TERMS

commercial paper, p. 153

draft, p. 153

promissory note, p. 154

certified check, p. 154

cashier's check, p. 154

Uniform Commercial Code (UCC), p. 155

accommodation party, p. 156

 JUMP START

Bernie Settleton bought a used Chevrolet Impala from Denise Phalan for $5,800. Settleton paid Phalan $300 down and promised to pay the remaining $5,500 with his tax refund check. A few days after the sale, Phalan bought a used, but newer, Chevrolet Impala from Dowdy's Cars. As partial payment to Dowdy's, Phalan drew a draft on the $5,500 Settleton owed her. To be sure Settleton had enough time to get the money, Phalan made the draft payable to the order of Dowdy's Cars 60 days after sight. Upon receiving the draft, Dowdy's Cars immediately presented it to Settleton. What should Settleton write on the check to indicate his willingness to pay in 60 days?

©George Dolgikh, 2009/Used under license from Shutterstock.com

Commercial Paper

The use of commercial paper—such as checks, drafts, and notes—developed over the last several centuries to relieve individuals of the need to carry large sums of gold, silver, or cash. It provided an alternate means of payment in the form of a piece of paper on which the owner of precious metals wrote an order requiring that a certain amount of those metals be transferred to the person named in the order. The order was addressed to an individual or a company who held such metals in safekeeping. That individual or company carried out the order after validating the signature as being that of the owner of the metals. This "paper" was the forerunner of the check.

Today's system is far more sophisticated, but a check still fulfills the same function. With a check, you order a financial institution in which you have deposited money to "pay to the order of" an individual or company. Electronic encoding is now used, but the basic use and purpose of checks hasn't changed.

Major Types of Commercial Paper

Commercial paper is defined as an unconditional written promise or order to pay a sum of money. *Unconditional*, as used to define commercial paper, means that the legal effectiveness of the order or promise does not depend on any other event. Commercial paper can be grouped into two categories—*orders* to pay money and *promises* to pay money. Drafts and checks are unconditional orders to pay money. Promissory notes and certificates of deposit are unconditional promises to pay money.

Drafts A **draft** or *bill of exchange* is an unconditional written order by one person that directs another person to pay money to a third. The person directed to pay may be a natural person or an artificial "legal" person, such as a corporation. If the nature of the transaction does not make it necessary to specify that a particular person receive the money, the order may be made payable to "cash" or to "bearer." Then any person in possession of the instrument may collect on it. The person who *executes*, or draws the draft and orders payment to be made, is the *drawer*. The *drawee* is the party ordered to pay the draft. The *payee* is the party to whom commercial paper is made payable. The drawee is usually the debtor of the drawer. *Acceptance* is the drawee's promise to pay the draft when due. Such a promise is usually evidenced by the signature of the acceptor (drawee) on the face of the instrument along with words indicating the acceptance.

Time of Payment Drafts are sometimes classified in terms of the time of payment. A draft may be payable "at sight," also termed as payable "on demand" or "at presentment." This is called a *sight draft*, which is presented to the drawee by the one holding the draft. The drawee on a sight draft is expected to pay immediately. If a draft is payable on a set date, at the end of a specified period after sight, or at the end of a specified period after the date of the draft, it is a *time draft*.

The time draft at the right was written because Joey Kleeman, the drawer, had just completed a construction job for Colyert Hardware, the drawee. Colyert owed Kleeman $6,500. The $6,500 was due and payable upon completion of the job. When B. A. Hill asked Kleeman for the $5,000 Kleeman owed him for backhoe work in the subdivision Kleeman was developing, Kleeman convinced him to take the draft instead. Hill then presented the instrument to Jim Colyert for acceptance. Colyert's "acceptance" is his assurance that he will be liable on the draft and will pay it according to its terms. Colyert has correctly indicated this by writing "accepted" and his signature across the instrument.

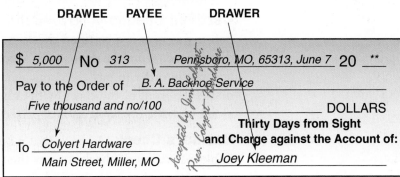

Checks A *check* is a type of draft a bank depositor uses to order the bank to pay money, usually to a third party. Checks usually are written on special forms that are magnetically encoded to simplify check processing. However, checks

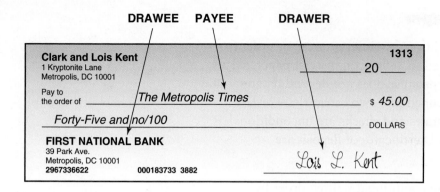

DRAWEE **PAYEE** **DRAWER**

Clark and Lois Kent
1 Kryptonite Lane
Metropolis, DC 10001

1313

_____ 20 ___

Pay to
the order of _____ The Metropolis Times _____ $ 45.00

Forty-Five and no/100 _____ DOLLARS

FIRST NATIONAL BANK
39 Park Ave.
Metropolis, DC 10001
2967336622   000183733 3882

Lois L. Kent

may be written on blank paper, on forms provided by the depositor, or on any other material and still be legally effective. The drawee, though, must always be a bank for the instrument to qualify as a check.

The bank agrees to *honor*, or pay when due, each check as long as sufficient funds are in the depositor's account. If sufficient funds are not present, the bank will usually *dishonor*, or refuse to pay when due, the instrument. When a check has been lost or stolen, the drawer can direct the bank not to pay it. Such an instruction is called a *stop-payment order*.

Promissory Notes A promissory note is an unconditional written promise by a person or persons to pay money according to the payee's order or to pay money to the bearer of the instrument. (See the illustration of a promissory note on p. 151.) The payment may have to be made on demand or at a definite time according to the stated terms on the note. The person who executes a promissory note is the *maker*. Two or more persons executing the note are termed "co-makers" and are both liable for payment.

Certificates of Deposit A *certificate of deposit (CD)* is an instrument bearing a bank's written acknowledgment of the receipt of money, together with an unconditional promise to repay it at a definite future time.

Specialized Types of Commercial Paper

The four types of commercial paper described above may come in various forms to meet specialized needs.

Certified Checks A personal check that has been accepted by a bank before payment is a certified check. At the time of certification, the bank draws funds from the depositor's account and sets them aside in a special account in order to pay the check when it is presented. In addition, the bank marks the front of the check with either the word "accepted" or "certified," along with the date and an authorized signature of the bank.

Cashier's Check A check that a bank draws on itself is a cashier's check. Banks use cashier's checks to pay their own obligations. People who need to pay others, but who do not have a checking account or cannot use their personal checks, may purchase cashier's checks from a bank. Because it is relatively risk-free, a payee usually is willing to accept a cashier's check from a person otherwise considered unreliable.

Teller's Check A draft drawn by a bank on funds that it has on deposit at another bank is a *teller's check*. Individuals and business firms may also use these instruments when a substantial sum is involved.

Money Orders Persons who do not have checking accounts often use money orders. A money order is a draft issued by a post office, bank, express company, or telegraph company for use in paying or transferring funds for the purchaser. For example, a money order purchased at one post office orders the post office at the location of the payee to make payment.

Traveler's Checks Travelers know that it is not safe to carry large sums of cash. The traveler's check was devised to overcome this problem. A traveler's check is a draft drawn by a well-known financial institution on itself or its agent. The buyer signs the traveler's checks when purchased. Later, when used to pay for a purchase, the traveler writes in the name of the payee and then signs again in the presence of the payee. The payee then deposits and collects the traveler's check in the same manner as other checks. The availability of automated teller machines (ATMs) in many foreign countries and problems with forgeries have reduced the use of traveler's checks considerably.

Trade Acceptances Like the check, the trade acceptance is a type of draft. It is written by the seller of goods, the drawer, on the money owed to him by the buyer of those goods, the drawee. If the buyer accepts the liability on the instrument, the seller has a valuable piece of commercial paper to sell.

Decreasing the Risk of Taking Commercial Paper

For people or businesses to accept commercial paper instead of cash, they must be assured that there is a very good chance the instrument will be paid. Today, the Uniform Commercial Code (UCC), a set of state laws that governs business activities, provides that assurance. To do this, the UCC empowers a qualified owner of commercial paper to overcome many of the legal defenses the person who is obligated to pay the instrument might raise to keep from paying.

To enable the owner to overcome most common defenses and collect on commercial paper, the promise or order to pay must be *negotiable*, or easily transferred. The requirements of a negotiable instrument include that it must be in writing, contain an unconditional promise or order payable in an amount that can be calculated from the face of the instrument, be payable on demand or at a definite time, and be payable to the bearer or to someone's order. It is also essential that the party trying to collect on it has acquired it in a proper manner. *Negotiation* means that a proper transfer of a negotiable instrument to a person wishing to collect on it has occurred.

Proper Transfer The proper method of transfer depends on whether the instrument is *order paper* (paper made payable to a specified payee) or *bearer paper* (paper made payable to "bearer," "cash," or any other way that does not identify a specific person). If the instrument is order paper, the named person or her or his agent must sign the paper on its reverse side and deliver it to the transferee. A signature on the back of an instrument is called an *indorsement*. The person who signs on the instrument's reverse side is known as an *indorser*. The party to whom the paper is indorsed is the *indorsee*. A party who has physical possession of commercial paper that is payable to his or her order or who is in possession of bearer paper is a *holder*. Therefore, a bearer is a holder, as is a person in possession of paper payable to his or her

TEAMWORK

In small groups, brainstorm situations in which each of the following types of commercial paper would be used: certified check, cashier's check, teller's check, money order, traveler's check, trade acceptance.

order. If the paper is bearer paper, it may be properly transferred and thereby negotiated by delivery alone.

Indorsements are classified by whether any words, other than the indorser's signature, have been added and, if so, what words. A *blank indorsement* consists of just the indorser's signature without any words added. Because it is quickly written, the blank indorsement is the most common. However, because it turns the paper into bearer paper, a thief or a finder of the paper may negotiate it.

A *special indorsement* makes the paper payable to the order of a named party. It requires the signature of the party named in the indorsement plus physical delivery to be properly negotiated. Transferees who receive commercial paper with blank indorsements may protect themselves by writing that the paper is payable to themselves above the indorser's signature. This is perfectly legal and restores the order character of the instrument. For example, Julia Sanchez could have taken the blank indorsement of Mario Sanchez and written above it "Pay to the order of Julia Sanchez" or "Pay to Julia Sanchez."

Blank Indorsement

Mario Sanchez

Special Indorsement

Pay to the order of Julia Sanchez

Mario Sanchez

If the maker or drawee of an instrument fails to pay it, the indorsers may be required to pay it. Adding words such as "not liable for payment" over a blank or special indorsement can eliminate this potential secondary liability based on signature. The result is a *qualified indorsement*.

Even though secondary liability is avoided by qualifying the indorsement, certain warranties still may bind a transferor. These warranties are implied by law against all transferors and may still require the indorser to pay if the instrument cannot be collected. The warranties guarantee that (1) the transferor is entitled to enforce the paper, (2) all signatures are genuine, (3) the instrument has not been altered, (4) the transferor has no knowledge of a bankruptcy proceeding against the maker, drawer of an unaccepted draft, or an acceptor, and (5) there are no defenses of any type that would be legally effective against the transferor.

A *restrictive indorsement* directs the use of the proceeds or imposes a condition upon payment. For example, "Pay to John Eric to be held in trust for his oldest son, Tommy," would be a restrictive indorsement, because it directs what is to be done with the proceeds of the paper. "For deposit only" and "for collection" also are restrictive indorsements.

Accommodation Parties Sometimes a person who desires to borrow money or to cash a check is not well known in the community or has not established credit. To make her or his commercial paper acceptable, the person might arrange for someone with good credit to cosign the paper. Such a cosigner is an **accommodation party**. Under such circumstances, the maker is still primarily liable. If the maker fails to honor the paper and the accommodation party is collected against, he or she has the right to seek compensation from the accommodated party.

Collection and Discharge of Commercial Paper

A holder of commercial paper has significant rights with regard to collection and discharge, but a *holder in due course* (HDC) has more. An HDC is a holder who takes the commercial paper in good faith, gives value for it, and does so without the knowledge of any defense, adverse claim to, or dishonor of the instrument. If a person cannot qualify as an HDC, he or she could still acquire the rights of an HDC as a *holder through a holder in due course* (HHDC). An HHDC is a holder who takes commercial paper after an HDC has held it. However, the UCC does not allow persons to improve their position on commercial paper through reacquisition of it. So a mere holder, who cannot qualify as an HDC, cannot acquire that status by transferring the paper to an HDC and reacquiring it from that party.

Collecting on Commercial Paper In collecting, an HDC or HHDC can overcome more of the defenses that the obligor on an instrument might raise against payment to a mere holder. Defenses that are good against everyone except an HDC or an HHDC are termed *limited defenses*. These defenses include breach of contract, failure of consideration, temporary legal incapacities (excluding minority), ordinary duress, prior payment or cancellation, unauthorized completion, and a few others. Defenses that are good against all plaintiffs suing on a negotiable instrument are called *universal defenses*. These defenses include the paper being consumer paper (issued for a consumer transaction, such as a promissory note or check given as payment for a person's car), illegalities, permanent incapacities, minority, and a few others.

Discharge of Commercial Paper Although the liability for the majority of commercial paper is eliminated, or discharged, by payment, other methods or circumstances also have the same effect. Cancellation, for example, consists of any act by the current holder that indicates intent to end the obligation (such as purposely—not accidentally—burning a promissory note). A fraudulent change to or completion of commercial paper by a party to the instrument also will discharge the obligation of the other party. If a holder extends the time of payment, releases the principal debtor, or impairs collateral provided as security for payment, any party whose rights are affected and who did not consent is discharged. Finally, a negotiable instrument may be discharged in the same ways as an ordinary contract for the payment of money. For example, a discharge could occur by *novation*, in which one party releases the other by agreeing to accept payment or performance from a substitute party. A discharge also may occur by *accord and satisfaction*, or by operation of law, such as in bankruptcy or with the statute of limitations.

COMMUNICATE

Practice writing the following types of check indorsements: blank, special, qualified, and restrictive. Exchange your indorsements with a partner and compare them.

CheckPOINT

Name the four major types of commercial paper.

_____

_____

Electronic Funds Transfers

A transfer of funds that requires a financial institution to debit or credit an account and that is initiated by the use of an electronic terminal, computer, telephone, or magnetic tape is an *electronic funds transfer (EFT)*. EFTs are conducted without paper instruments such as checks or drafts. ATMs, point-of-sale terminals in stores, pay-by-phone systems, and automated clearinghouse networks that credit payroll checks directly to employees' accounts are examples of devices that facilitate EFTs.

Since commercial paper law emphasizes the need for written documentation, the federal government enacted the Electronic Fund Transfer Act (EFTA) to protect consumers making such transfers. The EFTA emphasizes that the use of such transfers is to be purely voluntary. When an EFT is used, the consumer must immediately receive a written receipt and later must receive a statement of all transfers. If the consumer detects an error, it must be reported to the responsible institution within 60 days of the statement date. The institution then has 10 business days to investigate and report the results in writing. If the institution needs more time, it can use up to 45 days, but must meanwhile make the funds in dispute available to the consumer.

In the case of unauthorized transfers, Congress chose to divide the risk between the consumer and the financial institution. If notification is given to the financial institution within two business days of learning of the loss or theft of the debit card, the consumer is responsible only for the lesser of $50 or the value obtained in unauthorized transfers prior to the notification. If more than two days have elapsed before notification, the consumer may be responsible for up to a maximum of $500. However, if notification is not given within 60 days, the consumer may be fully liable.

How are consumers protected in EFT transactions?

©Rafael Ramirez Lee, 2009/Used under license from Shutterstock.com

CheckPOINT

What is an electronic funds transfer (EFT)?

_____

_____

Think Critically

1. Why do you think commercial paper is important in today's world?

_____

_____

_____

2. What is the difference between a promissory note and a certificate of deposit?

_____

_____

_____

3. Is using a trade acceptance a better business practice than supplying goods to retailers on account? Why or why not?

_____

_____

_____

4. What guidelines do you think were used to separate limited from universal defenses? Could you suggest another basis? If so, what is it?

_____

_____

_____

Make Academic Connections

5. **Communication** Use the Internet to locate banks in Switzerland, the Cayman Islands, and Singapore. Compare the advantages of the accounts, checking and otherwise, that they offer to the same types of accounts offered by U.S. banks. What are the differences, and why do you think these differences exist? Write a report on your findings.

6. **Research** Determine the relative importance of commercial paper to U.S. currency by researching how much currency is exchanged each day. Compare that amount to the amount of commercial paper exchanged. Is having an adequate supply of both important to our economy? Why or why not?

7. **Geography** Using spreadsheet software, chart how the exchange rates for currencies have gone up and down over the past 65 years. Use various countries from each continent but be sure to include countries devastated by World War II, such as Japan and Germany.

GOALS

Explain why secured transactions are necessary

Describe how a security interest is created and enforced

KEY TERMS

secured transaction, p.160

collateral, p. 160

termination statement, p. 163

 JUMP START

Patrick loaned his friend Chitra $500 cash for a down payment on a custom-made computer especially outfitted for online gaming. Chitra financed the remaining $1,500 of the purchase price through the seller, Max Out Computers, giving the retailer a security interest in the computer. Later, Chitra stopped making payments to Max Out while she still owed Max Out $600 and Patrick the $500. The retailer repossessed the computer and resold it for $900. Would Patrick get a share of the $900 as payment for the $500 he loaned Chitra? Why or why not?

Security Interests

During the Middle Ages, charging any interest on loans was illegal. Later in history, Hamlet's Polonius wisely counseled "neither a borrower nor a lender be." In contrast, debt is almost a necessity for today's average citizen to maintain the American way of life.

A *debtor* is a person or a business that owes money, goods, or services to another. Whatever is owed is called the *debt*. The *creditor* is the one to whom the debt is owed. If a creditor wants more assurance of repayment than just the mere word or written promise of the debtor, the creditor may ask for a secured transaction. A **secured transaction** is a legal device that creates a security interest in personal property or fixtures. A security interest is the interest in or claim against the debtor's property created for the purpose of assuring payment or performance of a debt or other obligation. **Collateral** is the property that is subject to the security interest of the creditor.

In a secured transaction, if the debtor defaults by failing to pay as promised, the creditor may exercise the legal *right of repossession*. This means the creditor may take the property named as collateral, sell it, and use the proceeds to pay the balance due. If the proceeds exceed the amount due, the difference is given to the debtor. If there is still a remaining balance due on the debt after the sale, the seller can sue the debtor to collect the remaining amount due. Creditors, be they sellers on credit or lenders of money, are more likely to be paid if they are secured parties. A *secured party* is the person or business with security interest in specific collateral owned by the debtor.

In contrast, a creditor holding a defaulted *unsecured* claim must first sue, get a court judgment, and then enforce that judgment against the debtor's property. Also, without the security interest, other creditors of the debtor may have equal or superior rights in such property. Worse still, if the debtor's financial obligations are discharged in bankruptcy, the unsecured creditor, is likely to receive nothing or only a few cents for each dollar of the unpaid debt.

Creation of a Security Interest

A security interest is created when three things take place. First, there must be an agreement between the debtor and creditor that the creditor will have a security interest. Second, the creditor must give value in return for the security interest. Third, the debtor, after the security interest is instituted, must retain rights (either ownership or possession) in the collateral. These three things can occur in any order. When all three have occurred, the security interest becomes enforceable against the debtor.

Types of Secured Transactions

There are two types of secured transactions. In a *pledge*, the creditor is given possession of the collateral. Leaving personal property with a pawn shop as collateral for an interest-bearing loan is an example of a pledge. If the loan is not repaid, the pawn shop can sell the property to cover the amount due.

In a *security agreement*, the debtor retains possession of the collateral. The security agreement must be in writing, must clearly identify the collateral, and must be signed by the debtor. Buying an automobile, major kitchen appliance, or other costly item on credit with the purchased items named as collateral are examples of security agreements. The debtor gets immediate possession and use of the goods. The seller, bank, or finance company that lends the money has the right to take the goods back if the debtor fails to make payments.

Perfection of a Security Interest

A perfected or fully enforceable security interest results when the creditor gives proper notice of its existence to all other potential creditors. Such notice may be given in a number of ways. A creditor in possession of the collateral, as in a pledge, needs to take no additional steps for protection. Possession alone is notice to any possible subsequent buyer or creditor that a security interest may exist. The creditor who has possession thereby has a perfected security interest. If a creditor is able to repossess collateral upon default, the act of retaking possession also perfects the security interest.

When the debtor has possession of the goods, it may be necessary for the creditor to file a financing statement at the appropriate governmental office to perfect the creditor's interest. A *financing statement* is a brief, written notice of the existence of a security interest in the identified property. Filing a financing statement gives *constructive notice* that a security interest in specific property exists. This means that the law presumes everyone has knowledge of the facts on file. Anyone concerned may get actual notice by checking the public records.

Perfection in Tangible and Intangible Property

Special provisions for perfecting the security interest depend on whether the property in question is tangible or intangible.

Tangible Property When tangible property is used as collateral, the procedure for perfecting the creditor's security interest depends on the type of goods, as follows.

- **Consumer goods** No filing of a financing statement is required to perfect a creditor's security interest in consumer goods, which are used primarily for personal, family, or household purposes. The obtaining of a proper security agreement by the lender or seller is sufficient.
- **Farm products** In most states, a filing of a financing statement is required to perfect a security interest in farm products, which include crops, livestock, unmanufactured products of the farm, and farm supplies.
- **Inventory** A filing is required to perfect a security interest in inventory, which includes business goods that are intended for sale or lease, raw materials, work in process, and materials used or consumed in a business.
- **Equipment** A filing is required to perfect a security interest in equipment, which includes goods used by a business in performing its function, such as telephone equipment or computers.

Intangible Property The procedure used in perfecting a security interest in intangible property depends on the classification of that property. A security

TEAMWORK

With a partner, role-play a situation in which one partner, the debtor, buys property of value from the other partner, the creditor. Make up the specific details of the transaction. Then write a financing statement that verifies the existence of the security interest in the property.

interest in accounts receivable or contractual rights that cannot be possessed in a physical sense must be perfected by filing unless the transaction does not cover a significant part of the debtor's accounts receivable or other contractual rights. For documents used in bailments, such as bills of lading, air bills, and warehouse receipts, the creditor may either file a financing statement or take possession of the goods upon default. To perfect a security interest in commercial paper, possession by the creditor upon default is essential.

Termination of a Secured Transaction

Most secured transactions are routinely terminated when the debtor pays the debt in full and the creditor releases the security interest in the collateral. If the creditor has filed a financing statement, this release is made when the creditor files a **termination statement**. This acknowledges the full payment of the debt to the governmental office that holds the financing statement. Filing the termination statement informs potential buyers and creditors that the property is no longer collateral. For consumer goods, the termination statement must be filed within 30 days of the payoff, or within 10 days of a written request by the debtor. Otherwise, the creditor must pay to the debtor $100 plus any loss caused to the debtor as a result of the untimely filing.

If the debtor defaults on the loan, the secured creditor who does not have possession of the collateral may take possession of it. This may be done without legal proceedings, provided it does not involve a breach of the peace. Even when in default as to payment, the debtor does not give up all rights. For example, the debtor may pay the balance due and the related expenses of the creditor and redeem the collateral any time before the creditor has resold it.

How can a secured creditor collect on a bad debt?

©SVLumagraphica, 2009/Used under license from Shutterstock.com

As an alternative to resale, the secured creditor may retain the collateral in full settlement of the debt. Written notice of the creditor's intention to keep the collateral must be given to the debtor. If the debtor, or any other person entitled to receive notice, objects in writing within 21 days, the creditor must dispose of the collateral in a reasonable manner by public or private sale.

Additional protection is given to consumers who have paid 60 percent or more. In such a situation, the creditor may not keep the collateral unless the consumer agrees in writing. In the absence of such a written agreement, the creditor must, in a commercially reasonable manner, sell the collateral within 90 days after the repossession and give to the debtor any proceeds that exceed what he or she owes.

CheckPOINT

What is the function of a termination statement?

_____

_____

Think Critically

1. Why is debt very important in our society? Why is the secured transaction an important means of financing purchases?

_____

_____

_____

2. In the last 50 years, the maximum time available to finance the purchase of an automobile has gone from 24 to 72 months. What do you think has caused this change? What are the effects of such a change?

_____

_____

_____

_____

3. Why does the perfection of security interests in consumer goods not require a filing?

_____

_____

_____

4. What kind of harm can be done if a creditor fails to file a termination statement after a large secured debt has been paid?

_____

_____

_____

Make Academic Connections

5. **Ecology** Does the ability to buy more now rather than in the future have an effect on the ecological systems of the planet? Is the effect positive or negative? Write a one-page position statement answering these questions.

6. **Marketing** Evaluate the points of competition between pawn shops. Look for ads for pawn shops in the phone book and local media. Do they mention specialty areas for the various shops, such as electronic goods or farm equipment? Contact the shops and request their interest rate schedules. Report to the class your evaluations.

JUMP START

Maria was the surety on a debt Ben owed to Chris. When Ben failed to pay on the due date, Chris graciously told Ben that he could pay the debt with his next month's paycheck. Chris thus extended the time for payment without notifying and getting Maria's consent. If Ben later defaults and goes bankrupt, can Chris legally force payment of the debt by Maria? Why or why not?

GOALS

Discuss the laws protecting creditors and debtors

List the types of bankruptcy and explain the bankruptcy procedure

KEY TERMS

suretyship, p. 166

garnishment, p. 166

©Edw, 2009/ Used under license from Shutterstock.com

Protection of Creditors and Debtors

In addition to the UCC protections surrounding secured transactions and the use of commercial paper, the law offers other shields to the risks involved in the financial dealings between debtors and creditors. These include the bankruptcy statutes, various state and federal agency rules, and some important common law provisions.

Laws Protecting Creditors

Laws protecting creditors that have their origin in the common law include various involuntary liens, third party assurances, and garnishment.

Involuntary Liens   Although most liens (the legal claim against another's property) are created with the consent of the debtor, statutes in many states create liens in favor of the creditor without such consent. These *involuntary liens* include the mechanic's lien and the artisan's lien.

   The *mechanic's lien* especially applies to the fields of construction and home improvement. It allows a person who has not been paid for labor or materials furnished for a project to file a legal claim against the real property involved. If the debt is not paid, the realty may be sold and the proceeds used to pay off the lien. The lienholder is entitled to the sale proceeds before other claimants, such as a bank with a mortgage on the property.

The *artisan's lien* allows persons who have not been paid for services, such as repairing a car or a computer, to retain possession of the personal property involved until payment is received. If payment is not made, the property may be sold to pay the debts that are due. Similar retention liens benefit other service providers. *Hotelkeepers' liens* allow the retention of a guest's possessions, such as luggage and jewelry, until payment is made for rental on or damages to the room. After a legally prescribed time, the goods may be sold to satisfy the debt. Note, however, that any lienholder who gives up possession of the property before the debtor pays for the services loses their lien.

Third Parties A creditor who wishes assurance beyond the debtor's promise to pay may demand that a creditworthy third party assume a form of responsibility for the liability. One such form is a suretyship. In a suretyship, the third party, called a *surety*, agrees to be primarily liable for the debt or obligation if payment or performance becomes overdue. Because the surety is primarily liable, the creditor does not have to show that the principal debtor cannot or would not pay the debt before collecting against the surety. Another form involving a third-party obligor brought in to protect the creditor is the *guaranty relationship*. In it, the third party, the *guarantor*, agrees to pay if the principal debtor fails to do so. Since the guarantor is only secondarily liable, the creditor must show that the primary obligor cannot be collected upon before collecting against the guarantor.

Garnishment of Wages Once a creditor's claim is shown to be legally valid and fair in a court hearing, the court may order that the debtor's wages be garnished. With garnishment, a portion of the debtor's wages is withheld by the employer and paid directly to the creditor. However, the total amount that can be garnished by all creditors is limited by the Consumer Credit Protection Act (CCPA) to 25 percent of the debtor's take-home pay (not including garnishments for child support).

Laws Protecting Debtors

There are six important types of laws designed to protect debtors.

Maximum Interest Rates Usury laws that set maximum interest rates were discussed in Chapter 2 on contracts. Usually, such laws apply only to loans of money. They do not govern additional charges added to the asking price because payment in full was not made at the time of the sale. These "carrying charges" are looked upon by the law as the means used in determining the final price of the goods and not as interest on a loan of money to buy them.

Clear and Complete Advance Disclosure of Loan Terms The federal Truth in Lending Act, part of the CCPA, was designed to protect consumers when they become debtors. The law applies only to consumer loans made for personal, household, family, or agricultural purposes. It does not limit the percentage amount that may be charged but requires a full disclosure of any interest and finance charges. For comparison purposes between loans, such charges must also be expressed as an annual percentage rate (APR).

Terms of Unconscionable Contracts Recall that an unconscionable contract is one that is grossly unfair and oppressive. It is typically a result of the unequal bargaining power of one party who makes a take-it-or-leave-it offer to another party who has no viable market alternative. Such a contract can sometimes be found in the extortionate charges for emergency repairs for stranded motorists. When confronted with such a contract, a judge may refuse to enforce it, may enforce the contract without the unconscionable clause, or may reduce the abusive charges or applications to acceptable limits.

Specific Abuses of the Credit System The Federal Equal Credit Opportunity Act makes it unlawful for any creditor to discriminate against an applicant because of gender or marital status. The Federal Fair Debt Collection Practices Act makes illegal any abusive and deceptive debt-collection practices, such as abusive language, threats of violence, third-party contacts, and communication with the debtor at work. The Federal Fair Credit Reporting Act regulates credit rating reporting companies. The Credit Repair Organizations Act governs the claims made and services provided by those who would work on your behalf to repair your credit standing. Finally, federal law requires that the debtor's liability for the unauthorized use of a credit card be limited to $50 or less, depending on when notification is given to the credit card company.

©Jason Stitt, 2009/ Used under license from Shutterstock.com

Notice of Debt Payment When a secured consumer debt is paid in full, the law allows the debtor to require the creditor to file notice of the payoff in the public record. If the creditor fails to do so within the proper time frame, monetary penalties will be imposed. Whether or not the debt is secured, debtors should always request payment receipts, especially for cash payments.

What are some of the laws protecting credit card users?

Cancellation of Debts Bankruptcy laws have been enacted to help debtors who have become overburdened with debts. In addition, state statutes of limitations require that efforts to enforce outstanding debts must cease after a certain time period, such as 3 to 6 years. Obligations in writing may be enforced for up to 6 years and court judgments for 20 years.

CheckPOINT

How does a suretyship differ from a guaranty relationship?

_____

_____

Bankruptcy Law

The U.S. Congress has exclusive power to establish uniform laws on bankruptcies. Bankruptcy law has two purposes. It protects debtors by giving them a new economic start free from most creditors' claims. It also protects creditors by setting up a framework to provide for the fair distribution of the debtor's assets. The Bankruptcy Abuse Prevention and Consumer Protection Act (BAPCPA) was recently placed in effect due to the high number of bankruptcies and consumer abuse burdening the previous bankruptcy statute.

What are the two purposes of bankruptcy law?

Types of Bankruptcy

Current Bankruptcy Code, which incorporates the BAPCPA changes, provides the following forms of possible relief for debtors.

Chapter 7 Liquidation Chapter 7 bankruptcy, also called *straight bankruptcy*, involves the sale for cash of the nonexempt property of the debtor and the distribution of the proceeds to creditors. Nonexempt property includes such assets as bank accounts, stocks, and bonds. Liquidation of these assets under Chapter 7 results in the discharge of the majority of the debtor's financial obligations. This is the most used form of bankruptcy.

Chapter 11 Reorganization This relief is designed to keep a corporation, partnership, or sole proprietorship in active business with no liquidation. The debtor or a committee of creditors files a plan for reorganization with the bankruptcy court. The court then reviews the plan. The creditors vote on the plan prior to the court's approval. The BAPCPA has added a streamlined Chapter 11 process for small businesses with debts not exceeding $2 million.

Chapter 13 Extended-Time Payment Plan Chapter 13 relief is available to individuals who have regular income and wish to avoid liquidation of their assets. The petitioning debtor must not have unsecured debts over $336,900 nor secured debts over $1,010,650 (limits subject to adjustment every three years). The debtor must submit a plan for the installment payment of debts over three years with a possible extension to five years.

Chapter 12 Plan Congress added Chapter 12 relief to the Bankruptcy Code in 1986 for family farm owners (excludes large agricultural operators) and family fishermen. The plan is almost identical to Chapter 13, except the debt limits range from $1.5 to $3.5 million.

Voluntary or Involuntary Bankruptcy

Liquidation under Chapter 7 of the Bankruptcy Act may be voluntary or involuntary. With few exceptions, any person, business, or other association may request *voluntary bankruptcy*. A person does not have to be insolvent or unable to pay debts to file voluntary bankruptcy. With some exceptions, any person or business owing $11,625 or more and unable to pay debts may be forced into *involuntary bankruptcy* by 1 to 11 petitioning unsecured creditors. If there are 12 or more creditors, at least 3 must sign the petition.

BANKRUPTCY IN GREAT BRITAIN

Bankruptcy laws in the United States are more lenient than those in other countries. The laws concerning bankruptcy reorganization in Great Britain, for example, assume that a company's financial problems are based solely on mismanagement. A team of bankruptcy accountants is assembled to handle the company's reorganization and sale of its assets.

Think Critically

What would be the benefit of strict bankruptcy laws to a country? What would be the downside? Which type of bankruptcy laws, strict or lenient, do you think are preferable? Explain your answer.

Bankruptcy Procedure In all bankruptcy proceedings, the debtor must file a list of all creditors with amounts owed, a list of all property owned, a statement explaining his or her financial affairs, and a list of current income and expenses. After the petition is filed, a trustee is selected. The trustee's duties are to find and to protect the assets of the debtor, liquidate them, and pay the claims against the debtor's estate with the proceeds.

Nondischargeable Debts Certain types of claims cannot be discharged by bankruptcy. These include certain taxes, alimony and child support, and claims for property obtained by fraud, embezzlement, or larceny. Judgments against the debtor for willful and malicious injury to the person or property of another, student loans owed to the government or to a nonprofit school of higher learning, judgments against the debtor resulting from driving while intoxicated, and any claims not listed by the debtor also are not dischargeable.

Exempt Property Certain assets of the debtor are exempt from seizure and liquidation. Individual states are permitted to substitute their own exemptions. The law also allows the petitioner to choose between state and federal exemptions. Under federal law, exempt property includes the following (with values subject to revision every three years).

- Up to $15,000 in equity in the debtor's home
- Up to $2,950 interest in one motor vehicle
- Up to $1,850 interest in the debtor's tools of trade
- Alimony and child support payments, social security payments, and welfare and pension benefits
- Up to $475 per item of household goods and furnishings, wearing apparel, books, animals, crops, and musical instruments (not to exceed $9,850)
- Up to $1,225 in jewelry

Liquidation and Distribution of Proceeds Assets of the debtor not subject to a security interest are liquidated by the trustee. The proceeds are

TEAMWORK

In small groups, collect and compare the bankruptcy exemption lists of at least five states. Share the results of your work with the class

Use Your Judgment

The Richmonds were almost $20,000 in debt. Nearly 90 percent of it was owed to credit card companies. The trustee in the Richmond's filing for Chapter 7 liquidation pointed out to the court that the Richmond's listing of their monthly expenses included voluntary payments to support their grandchildren. If these payments were stopped and applied to their debts, nearly all of the Richmond's credit card debt could be paid off in 36 months. As a consequence, the trustee filed a motion to dismiss the Richmond's case as an abuse of the bankruptcy laws.

THINK CRITICALLY
How do you think the bankruptcy court judge should rule? Given the trustee's analysis, under what other bankruptcy law should the Richmonds have filed?

used to pay the creditors. If a secured creditor's sale of the property exceeds the value of the security interest, the remainder is paid into the liquidation fund. If the sale does not cover the amount owed, the secured party can file against the other liquidation proceeds as a general creditor. The following is the order of priority for payout of the liquidation funds to claimants of general interest.

1. Unsecured claims for domestic support orders

2. Administrative expenses, such as court costs and trustee's and attorney's fees

3. Unpaid wages, salaries, and commissions up to a maximum of $10,950 per creditor

4. Contributions to employee benefit plans up to $10,950 per employee

5. Claims, up to $2,425 per claim, for unsecured deposits with the debtor for purchase or lease of property or for contracted services not provided

6. Unsecured claims of governmental units for taxes and penalties

7. Claims of all general unsecured creditors and those with residual unsatisfied claims from categories with higher priorities

If any amount is left after all the above claimants have been satisfied, it is turned over to the debtor. All eligible debts of the debtor are considered discharged. The debtor cannot file a bankruptcy petition again until six years have elapsed. Bankruptcy stays on a credit report for 10 years.

CheckPOINT

Give five examples of exempt property under federal bankruptcy law.

_____

_____

Think Critically

1. Why is it necessary for the debtor's property to be in the possession of the creditor/artisan for the artisan's lien to be effective? What must the artisan do if she or he gives up possession and is not paid?

_____

_____

_____

_____

2. Do the laws governing debtor–creditor protections seem consistent? Why or why not?

_____

_____

_____

_____

3. Dollar amounts in the bankruptcy statutes are subject to adjustment every three years based on the consumer price index. Do you agree with Congress's decision for such adjustment? Why or why not?

_____

_____

_____

_____

Make Academic Connections

4. **Research** Find out how many individuals file bankruptcy every month in your federal jurisdiction. Interview local lenders and ask them what provision they make for uncollectible debts. Report your findings to the class.

5. **Government** Search the Internet for information on the Consumer Credit Protection Act. Find out when this law was enacted and what, besides Truth in Lending, the Act regulates. Outline the important components of this Act.

6. **Agriculture** The Chapter 12 plan for bankruptcy covers "family farm owners" but excludes companies that run large agricultural operations. Why do you think Congress passed this plan? Do you think it was fair to exclude the farmers who own large agricultural enterprises? Why or why not? Use word processing software to write a paragraph explaining your answer.

Chapter Summary

6.1 **Commercial Paper**

A. Drafts, checks, promissory notes, and certificates of deposit are types of commercial paper in common use.

B. Electronic funds transfers are initiated by use of an electronic terminal, computer, telephone, or magnetic tape. They involve a financial institution debiting or crediting a user's account.

6.2 **Secured Transactions**

A. Secured transactions cut down greatly on the risk of issuing credit and, therefore, make credit cheaper for borrowers in the long run.

B. A proper secured transaction must involve creating a security interest in the property of the debtor.

6.3 **Debtor–Creditor Rights**

A. Laws protecting creditors allow involuntary liens, third-party suretyships and guaranty relationships, and garnishment of wages. Laws protecting debtors set maximum interest rates, require full disclosure of terms, change or void unconscionable contracts, correct abuses, require notice of debt payoff, and allow overburdened debtors to declare bankruptcy.

B. During bankruptcy procedure, a petition is filed, a trustee is selected, nonexempt assets are sold, the proceeds are used to pay creditors, and the court discharges the remaining debt.

Vocabulary Builder

Choose the term that best fits the definition. Write the letter of the answer in the space provided. Some terms may not be used.

_____ 1. State laws regulating business activities

_____ 2. An unconditional written order by one person that directs another person to pay money to a third

_____ 3. A check that a bank draws on itself

_____ 4. A person with good credit who acts as a cosigner

_____ 5. An unconditional written promise to pay money to another according to the terms of the instrument

_____ 6. A third party agrees to be primarily liable for another's debts

_____ 7. Property that is subject to the security interest of the creditor

_____ 8. A legal device that creates a security interest in personal property or fixtures

_____ 9. An acknowledgment of full payment of a debt to the governmental office that has the related financing statement

_____ 10. An unconditional written promise or order to pay a sum of money

a. accommodation party

b. cashier's check

c. certified check

d. collateral

e. commercial paper

f. draft

g. garnishment

h. promissory note

i. secured transaction

j. suretyship

k. termination statement

l. Uniform Commercial Code (UCC)

Review Concepts

Point Your Browser
www.cengage.com/
school/business/21biz

11. Name six different types of commercial paper.

_____

_____

12. How does a person become a holder in due course?

_____

_____

_____

13. Name the requirements for negotiability.

_____

_____

_____

_____

14. Explain the difference between a blank and a special indorsement.

_____

_____

_____

15. What are the requirements for a security agreement?

_____

_____

16. What are the categories of tangible goods used for collateral?

_____

_____

17. List three examples of intangible goods that can be used as collateral.

_____

_____

18. Name three types of involuntary liens and describe how each handles unpaid debts.

_____

_____

_____

19. List five types of debts that cannot be discharged in bankruptcy.

_____

_____

_____

_____

Apply What You Learned

20. A mere holder, who cannot qualify as an HDC, cannot acquire that status by transferring the paper to an HDC and reacquiring it from that party. Why does the UCC not allow a person to improve his or her position as a holder in this way?

_____

_____

_____

_____

21. What is the purpose of giving notice of a security interest's existence?

_____

_____

_____

22. Can you think of any tangible or intangible goods that cannot be used as collateral?

_____

_____

_____

_____

23. Should we allow human organs, blood, or other bodily fluids to be collateral? Why or why not?

_____

_____

_____

_____

24. For what type of transactions are credit or debit cards more suitable than currency? Why?

_____

_____

_____

_____

25. Could knowledge be considered collateral? If not, why not? If so, under what circumstances?

_____

_____

_____

_____

Make Academic Connections

26. **Environment** Under what circumstances would water be considered collateral? How about the air and/or sunshine? Is this a good or a bad idea? Write a paragraph explaining your views on this issue.

27. **Entertainment Law** Bondholders often hold the key in potential bankruptcy reorganizations and liquidations, and such seems to be the case with MGM studios, which is currently saddled with over $3 billion in debt. The famous 80-plus-year-old movie production house recently issued a plea to its bondholders for $20 million in short-term loans to cover overhead and for $150 million to complete or initiate several projects. Bondholders are reportedly reluctant and would rather see the studio go through a Chapter 11 reorganization. However, expert opinion says that MGM could lose its rights to the *James Bond 007* film series in such a restructuring. Further, it would delay the filming of *The Hobbit*, a potential blockbuster. If you were an MGM bondholder, what factors would you consider in reaching a decision on this matter? Would you extend the necessary funds or recommend Chapter 11? Explain your answer.

_____

_____

_____

_____

28. **Marketing** Go to your library and read newspapers from various parts of the country. Compare the level of sophistication and subject matter in the financial ads. Research the various ways the financial centers communicate with one another. Describe your observations in a short report.

Ethical Dilemma

29. MGM's motto from its founding has always been Ars Gratia Artis, which translates as "Art for Art's Sake." The motto circles the famed roaring lion shown at the beginning of its films and has been reflected over the years in the lavish wardrobes, expensive sets, and leading stars featured in its films. American culture looks back to MGM productions such as *Gone with the Wind* and *The Wizard of Oz* with nostalgia. If you were one of the bondholders referred to in Question 27, would you feel a moral obligation to preserve a studio with such a heritage, especially in a time when many traditional American businesses are disappearing? Why or why not?

_____

_____

_____

_____

GLOSSARY

A

Acceptance agreement by an offeree to the terms of the offer (p. 42)

Accommodation party cosigner of a loan who has a good credit rating (p. 156)

Agency relationship in which one party may legally bind the other by words or actions (p. 94)

B

Bailment the temporary transfer of possession and control of personal property subject to an agreement that typically calls for the subject property to be returned to the person creating the bailment at a later time or passed on to a specified third party (p. 77)

Boycott a refusal to do business with a particular person or firm in order to obtain concessions (p. 110)

Business judgment rule neither shareholders, directors, nor other officers can be held personally liable to parties outside the corporation for honest errors of judgment made in exercising their corporate powers (p. 140)

Business law the specific group of laws that regulates the establishment, operation, and termination of commercial enterprises (p. 4)

C

Case law law created by judicial branch of government (p. 14)

Cashier's check a check that a bank draws on itself (p. 154)

Certified check a personal check that has been accepted by a bank before payment (p. 154)

Civil law the group of laws within the common law that deal with wrongs against individual persons (p. 15)

Collateral the property that is subject to the security interest of the creditor (p. 160)

Collective bargaining negotiations over conditions and terms of employment between representatives of a work force and its employer (p. 110)

Commercial paper an unconditional written promise or order to pay a sum of money (p. 153)

Common law law based on current customs practiced by most of the people (p. 6)

Consideration what the offeror demands, and generally must receive, in order to make the offer legally enforceable against the offeror (p. 43)

Constitution a document that sets forth the framework of a government and its relationship to the people it governs (p. 10)

Contract an agreement between two or more parties that creates an obligation of some type (p. 32)

Copyright

Copyright protects the expression of a creative work such as the work of an author, artist, or composer (p. 83)

Corporation a legal entity or artificial person created through the authority of federal or state law (p. 134)

Court of record an exact account of what went on at trial (p. 22)

Criminal law governs offenses that violate citizens' right to live in peace (p. 15)

D

Deed document by which rights and interests in real property are transferred (p. 73)

Discrimination in employment hiring, promoting, or discharging on the basis of race, color, sex, religion, or national origin (p. 107)

Draft an unconditional written order by one person that directs another person to pay money to a third (p. 153)

E

Employment a relationship in which the employer pays the employee to do work under the control and direction of the employer (p. 100)

Estate bundle of rights (p. 73)

Ethical system a way of deciding what is right or wrong in a consistent, reasoned, impartial manner (p. 7)

Express contract contract with terms set down in a clear-cut fashion, either orally or in writing (p. 33)

F

Fiduciary duty in a partnership, a partner acting in good faith and putting the partnership interest above her or his own (p. 130)

Fraud reckless or intentional misrepresentation of an existing, important fact (p. 48)

Fringe benefits forms of payment not directly related to work performance (p. 101)

Fungible there is no difference between one unit of the goods and another (p. 79)

G

Garnishment a court-ordered method in which the employer withholds a portion of the debtor's wages and pays it directly to the creditor (p. 166)

General partnership an association of two or more persons to carry on a business for profit as co-owners (p. 126)

I

Implied contract contract with terms determined from the surrounding circumstances or an established pattern of dealings (p. 33)

Insurance a contractual obligation taken on by one party to indemnify the loss incurred by another party (p. 70)

Intellectual property intangible property that one cannot see or touch, including copyrights, patents, trade secrets, service marks, and trademarks (p. 83)

J

Jurisdiction the power to hear and decide cases (p. 19)

L

Labor union representative organization for employees that sets up bargaining procedures with employers (p. 110)

Laws rules of conduct that a political authority will enforce (p. 4)

Limited liability corporation (LLC) corporation that offers limited liability protection and taxation as a partnership (p. 143)

Limited liability partnership (LLP) form of business organization that offers ease of conversion from an existing partnership, avoidance of double taxation, and partial limited liability protection (p. 144)

Limited partnership made up of one or more general partners with full personal liability and one or more limited partners whose liability for partnership obligations extends only to the amount of their investment in the business (p. 127)

M

Misrepresentation an innocent misstatement of a significant fact by a party (p. 48)

N

Necessaries things needed to maintain life and lifestyle, such as food, clothing, or shelter (p. 46)

O

Offer proposal of a bargain or exchange to another party or parties (p. 35)

P

Patent a property right that excludes others from making, using, offering for sale, selling, or importing the invention (p. 85)

Personal property rights and interests in basically anything that is not real property, tangible or intangible (p. 65)

Power of attorney a written agency authorization (p. 95)

Promissory note an unconditional written promise by a person or persons to pay money according to the payee's order or to pay money to the bearer of the instrument (p. 154)

Property rights and interests in things that society allows people to claim (p. 64)

R

Ratification a person acts toward a contract as though he or she intends to be bound by it (p. 46)

Real property rights and interests in land, buildings, and fixtures (p. 65)

S

S corporation corporation organized under subchapter S of the Internal Revenue Code whose earnings are treated the same as a gain (or loss) from a partnership and taxed at the individual owner's level (p. 142)

Secured transaction a legal device that creates a security interest in personal property or fixtures (p. 160)

Shareholders owners of a corporation (p. 138)

Shares of stock units of ownership in a corporation (p. 134)

Sole proprietorship a business owned by one person (p. 122)

Statute of frauds a law that specifies the situations that require a writing (p. 55)

Statutes laws enacted by legislatures (p. 13)

Suretyship an agreement in which a third party (surety) is primarily liable for the debt or obligation of the debtor if payment or performance becomes overdue (p. 166)

T

Terminable at will employment contracts that either party can end without notice at any time without involving the courts (p. 101)

Termination statement release document that acknowledges the full payment of the debt that is sent to the governmental office holding the financing statement (p. 163)

Trade secret commercially valuable information that the owner attempts to keep secret (p. 86)

Trademark a word, mark, symbol, or device that identifies a product of a particular manufacturer or merchant (p. 84)

U

Unemployment compensation money paid to qualified workers who have lost their jobs (p. 114)

Unfair labor practices union or employer actions that violate the rights of employees with respect to union activity (p. 110)

Uniform Commercial Code (UCC) a set of state laws that governs business activities (p. 155)

Usury lending money at an interest rate higher than the maximum allowable rate set by state law (p. 52)

V

Valid contract contract that is legally binding and enforceable (p. 34)

INDEX

disabled employees, legislation in
   support of, 107
Equal Employment Opportunity
   Commission, 107
Equal Pay Act of 1963, 110–111
Fair Labor Standards Act (FLSA), 110
Family and Medical Leave Act
   (FAMLA), 111
individuals prohibited from
   working, 109
National Labor Relations Act
   (NLRA), 110
North American Agreement on Labor
   Cooperation, 112
North American Free Trade
   Agreement, 112
OSHA, 111
sexual harassment, 108
social insurance, 113–114
Government and public administration,
   as career, 2
Grantee, 73
Grantor, 73
Gratuitous agency, 96, 98
Gratuitous bailment, 79
Great Depression, The, 101
Guarantor, 166
Guaranty relationship, 166
Guardian, 47

H

Habitual drunkard, 47
Health insurance, 114
Heir, 66
Hinckley, John, 16
Holder, 155
Holder in due course (HDC), of
   commercial paper, 157
Holder through a holder in due course
   (HHDC), 157
Holdover tenant, 74
Homeowner's insurance, 70
Honor, commercial paper, 154
Hotelkeeper's lien, 166
Housing code, 74

I

Illegal acts, contract law and, 51
Illegal monopoly, 142
Impartial decisions, 7–8
Impartiality, 7–8
Impeachment cases, 23
Implied-at-law contract, 34
Implied authority, 95
Implied contract, 33
Incorporation, 138
Incorporation specification, 141
Indemnify, 70
Independent contractor, agency and, 95
Indorsee, 155–156

Indorsement, of commercial paper, 155–156
Indorser, 155–156
Inferior jurisdiction, 24
Information technology, as career, 30
Infringement, on copyrights, 84
Inheritance, acquiring property by, 66
Injury, on the job. *See* Safety, on the job
Insurable interest, 70
Insurance
   casualty, 70
   defined, 70
   life, 70
   social, 113–114
   types of, 70
Insured, 70
Insurer, 70
Intangible property, 162–163
Intellectual property, 65
   copyrights, 83–84
   defined, 83
Interest, usury and, 52
Internet
   cybercontracting and, 35
   cyberslacking and, 104
   free speech on, 21
   research current legislation on, 13
   Twittering the stock market, 136
Intestate, 66
Intoxication, contract law and, 47
Inventory, as tangible property, 162
Involuntary bailment, 80
Involuntary bankruptcy, 168
Involuntary liens, 165–166
iPod, as trademark, Apple, 84

J

Joint tenancy, 68
JP Morgan Chase, 150
Judicial branch of government, 13, 18–19
Jurisdiction
   appellate, 20, 22
   defined, 19
   inferior, 24
   original, 19–20
Justice, 6
Juvenile courts, 24
Juveniles, 24

K

Kindle, electronic reader, 162
King's Court, 5

L

Labor union, 110
Landlord, 73
Law(s)
   case law, 14
   classifications of
      civil, 15
      criminal, 15

procedural, 15
      substantive, 16
   defined, 4
   ethics and, 7
   finance and (project), 151
   growth of, 5
   government, employment regulations
      and, 106–117
         affirmative action plans, 108
         age discrimination, 108
         bona fide occupational
            qualifications, 109
         disabled employees, legislation
            in support of, 107
         Equal Employment Opportunity
            Commission, 107
         Equal Pay Act of 1963,
            110–111
         Fair Labor Standards Act
            (FLSA), 110
         Family and Medical Leave Act
            (FAMLA), 111
         individuals prohibited from
            working, 109
         National Labor Relations Act
            (NLRA), 110
         North American Agreement on
            Labor Cooperation, 112
         North American Free Trade
            Agreement, 112
         OSHA, 111
         sexual harassment, 108
         social insurance, 113–114
   how U.S. developed, 6
   protecting creditors, 165–166
   protecting debtors, 166–167
   sources of
      administrative agencies, 12–13
      constitutions, 10–12
      statutes, 13
Lawmaking powers, of branches of
   government, 13
Leasehold, 73
Legal procedures, obstruction of in
   contracts, 53
Legislative branch, of government, 13
Legislative power, 14
Legislatures, 14
Lessor, 73
Liability
   in business partnerships, 130
   in commercial paper, 156, 157
   vicarious, 103
Licenses, real property and, 75
Liens, involuntary, 165–166
Liens, types of, 165–166
Life estate, 73
Life insurance, 70
Limited defenses, in commercial
   paper, 157

Sports contracts, (Net Bookmark), 43
Stare decisis, 14, 15
State administrative agencies, 13–14
State constitutions
    power and, 13
    as sources of law, 10–11
State courts, 21–24
    associate circuit, 23
    courts of appeal, 22
    diagram, 23
    juvenile, 24
    municipal, 23
    probate, 24
    small claims, 24
    supreme, 22–23
    trial courts, 21–22
Statute of frauds, 55–56
Statutes, 13
Stock, shares of, in corporations, 134
Stock, types of, 139
Stock market, Twitter and, 136
Stop-payment order, on commercial
        paper, 154
Straight bankruptcy, 168
Strike, 110
Subletting, 74
Substantive law, 16
Superior courts, 22
Supreme Court, U.S. *See* U.S. Supreme
        Court (USSC)
Surety, 166
Survivor's insurance, 113
Symbol, of personal property, 78

T

Tangible property, 162
Tax numbers, 124
Teamwork
    agency relationships, 97
    bankruptcy exemptions, 169
    commercial paper, 155
    contracts, 33
    copyright, 84
    court systems, 20
    decision making, 7
    discrimination, 109
    fiduciary duty, 130
    find sources of laws, 15
    fringe benefits, 101
    fungible goods, 79
    investing in the stock
        market, 136
    juvenile courts, 24
    necessaries and nonnecessaries, 46
    offer role-play, 40
    property, 65
    restrictions on real property, 75
    secure interest in property, 162
    sole proprietorship, 123
    written contracts, 56

Tech Literacy
    Amazon Kindle, 162
    cybercontracting, 35
    cyberslacking, 104
    Digital Millennium Copyright Act
        (DMCA), 85
    freedom of speech, 21
    Twittering the stock market, 136
Teller's check, as commercial
        paper, 154
Tenancies, 73–74
Tenancy at sufferance, 74
Tenancy at will, 74
Tenancy by the entireties, 68
Tenancy for years, 73
Tenancy in common, 68
Tenancy in partnership, 129
Terminable at will, 101
Termination
        of employment contract, 103–104
        exceptions to at-will, 104
        notice of in agency, 98
        of a secured transaction, 163
Termination statement, 163
Test of the reasonable observer, 38–39
Testate, 66
Testator, 66
Testatrix, 66
Third parties, in debt protection, 166
Time draft, as commercial paper, 153
Time of payment, as commercial
        paper, 153
Title, to property, 64–65
Trade acceptance, as commercial paper, 155
Trade fixtures, 72
Trade secrets, 86
Trademark, 84–85
Transcript, of trial, 20
Traveler's check, as commercial
        paper, 155
Trespasser, 75
Trial court, 19
        state, 21–22
Trials in progress, visit, 3
Truth in Lending Act, 166–167
Twittering, the stock market, 136

U

UCC. *See* Uniformed Commercial Code
Unconditional commercial paper, 153
Unconscionability, 49
Unconscionable contract, 40, 167
Undue influence, in contract law, 48
Unemployment compensation, 114
Unemployment insurance, 114
Unfair labor practices, 110
Uniform Commercial Code (UCC), 155
Uniform Partnership Act (UPA), 1, 126–
        127, 129
Unilateral contract, 35–36

Unilateral mistakes of law, 47–48
Union, labor, 110
Universal defenses, in commercial
        paper, 157
Unsecured claim, 161
UPA. *See* Uniform Partnership Act
U.S. businesses overseas, 131
U.S. Constitution. *See* Constitution of the
        United States
U.S. copyright law, 85
U.S. Copyright Office, 84
U.S. Department of Justice, 2
U.S. District Courts, 19–20
U.S. laws
    development of, 6
    types of, 10–13
U.S. Patent and Trademark office, 85
U.S. Supreme Court (USSC), 18, 20–21
U.S. Tax Court, 19
USCC. *See* U.S. Supreme Court
Useful, patents, 86
Use Your Judgment
    assassination attempt on
        Reagan, 16
    bankruptcy, 170
    discrimination, 109
    incorporating partnerships, 137
    noncompete agreements, 55
    patents and trade secrets, 86
Usurious interest, 52
Usury, 52
Usury laws, 166

V

Valid contract, 34
Variances, real property and, 75
Vault.com, 104
Vicarious liability, 103
Vocational rehabilitation, 112
Void contract, 35
Voidable contract, 34
Voluntary bankruptcy, 168

W

Warranty deed, 73
Washington, George (President), 18
Whistleblowers, 104
Wills, 66
Winding up, partnerships, 132
Work, proper environment for, 102
Workers' compensation, 112–113
World of Warcraft, 62
Writing
    contract in, 33, 55–56
    obligations in, 167
Writ of certiorari, 20

Z

Zoning, 75